Voyages of Hope

The Saga of the Bride-Ships

Peter Johnson

TouchWood Editions Ltd. Victoria, BC, Canada.
This book is distributed by The Heritage Group, #108-17665 66A Avenue, Surrey,
BC, Canada, V3S 2A7.
http://www.touchwoodeditions.com

Cover and book design: Pat McCallum; layout by Retta Moorman; cover photo: self
portrait by Tania Strauss.

TouchWood Editions acknowledges the financial support for its publishing program
from The Canada Council for the Arts, the Government of Canada through the Book
Publishing Industry Development Program (BPIDP) and the Province of British Columbia
through the British Columbia Arts Council.

This book, set in Garamond, was printed and bound in Canada by Friesens, Altona, Manitoba.

National Library of Canada Cataloguing in Publication Data

Johnson, Peter Wilton
   Voyages of hope

   Includes bibliographical references and index.
   ISBN 0-920663-79-6

   1. Women immigrants—British Columbia—History—19th century. 2. Women
immigrants—British Columbia—Biography. 3. British Columbia—Emigration and
immigration—History—19th century. I. Title.
FC 3850.B7J63 2002   304.8'711041'082   C2002-910542-0
F1089.7.B7J63 2002

BRITISH
COLUMBIA
ARTS COUNCIL
Supported by the Province of British Columbia

The Canada Council | Le Conseil des Arts
for the Arts | du Canada

To the memory of
Bert and Margaret Sykes
emigrants on a latter-day bride-ship

Acknowledgments

Re-creating the narrative of the bride-ships saga through its twists and turns of time and place is akin to putting together a jig-saw puzzle in a dark room with half the pieces missing. Some sections, such as the outline of the story, are readily accessible and appear in several historical or scholarly sources. However, the details of the inner, more esoteric pieces were often due to dedicated public archivists and librarians, who guided me toward clues and interpretations from the most amazing sources.

Rachel Grant, Archivist and Librarian at the Vancouver Maritime Museum, was a treasure. She and Curator Emeritus, Leonard McCann, never flinched at my endless questions and directed me toward bits of information that became beacons of light in a sea of darkness. Doreen Stephens, Archivist for the Anglican Synod of British Columbia, provided me with useful history of the Columbia Mission Society, as did Bob Stewart, Archivist for the United Church of Canada. Thanks too to Joan Seidl of the Vancouver Museum, Vancouver, BC, Bill Quackenbush of the Barkerville Museum, Barkerville, BC, and Elsie Thorstvedt of the Norsk Siofartsmuseum, Oslo. Tony Cavanagh of Deakin University, Geelong, Australia, and Terry Berry of the Oldham Archives, Lancashire, England, were especially helpful. Ruth Greenbaum of the Manchester Art Gallery, Lynn Wright of the Maritime Museum of British Columbia (Victoria), David Mattison of the British Columbia Archives, Patrick Dunn of the University of British Columbia, Karen Cordiner, Louise Lavoie, Katie Gusola and Dick and Vivian Bevis all played a role.

Friends Rodger and Pat Touchie of Heritage House Publishing were always enthusiastic and kept me moving, as did Darlene Nickull. Editor Marlyn Horsdal of TouchWood Editions was ever patient with my scratchings, and more than any other, helped me be clear.

Whatever spaces or tentative interpretations still exist in this incomplete investigative report remain mine and mine alone.

Peter Johnson, 2002

Contents

Introduction
THE BRIDE-SHIPS AND THE *FILLES DU ROI*

When the *Marcella*, the *Tynemouth,* the *Robert Lowe* and the *Alpha* arrived in Victoria between 1862 and 1870, they brought over a hundred single women to the west coast. They were destined to become the wives not only of businessmen in the two colonies, but also of other workers, who burrowed feverishly into the muck of the gold-rich mountains. Many, as was the custom for unmarried women of the time, found shelter and service with the genteel aristocracy of Victoria. Others grew rich in infamy under gas-lights of a different kind. Their story is part of the shaping of this province; it is a tale of miners and murderers, of racism and respectability, of family and faith.

Gold brought the men, the men brought the missionaries and the missionaries brought the women. When gold fever hit the Fraser River in 1858, the race was on, not just to secure the yellow metal for personal fortunes but to secure a country. The gold camps along the Fraser River canyons grew into towns and showed unhappy signs of violence — a territory larger than France was at risk. The men must stay and settle down and the key to that colonial security, it was felt by many, was women.

It wasn't a new idea at all. Marriageable women had already been shipped out to New Orleans, to New Zealand and to the vast, empty continent of Australia. They had first been sent to Canada as the *Filles du Roi*, the "King's Daughters." Beginning in 1663, the French Crown paid the passage for over 800 single young women in a decade to emigrate to New France and become wives for the soldiers and settlers of France's colony in the New World. King Louis XIV promised each woman a dowry as soon as she married a member of the disbanded Carignan-Salieres regiment in Quebec City or one of the thousands of bachelor farmers throughout the colony. The *Filles du Roi* themselves readily agreed to keep the Catholic faith, raise families and essentially secure the fledgling colony of New France for a faraway crown.

There are some similarities between the *Filles du Roi* and the women of British Columbia's bride-ships. Both groups were caught up in the maelstrom of an unstable time at home. Many of the French emigrants were from the religious orphanages around Paris while many of the British were from Anglican orphanages around London. Most were young girls, barely in their teens. Both groups were sponsored and most of the girls had their passage paid for by powerful religious and humanitarian agencies. Their respective voyages out to the New World were equally fraught with terror and when they arrived, all the women were wards of an overly intrusive colonial government. Most of those eligible married, and only a few chose the single life; some prospered, some encountered heart-wrenching tragedy, while others were reduced to derelict and degraded lives. Many of their descendants are alive and thriving in Quebec and British Columbia today. The resemblances, however, end there.

The men that the women of British Columbia's bride-ships came to marry were not peasant farmers who wished only to settle down, work the land and worship as they had done in Europe for centuries. The pioneers on this coast had different fires in their bellies.

The experiment in social engineering that sent the bride-ships to British Columbia was doomed from the outset. The single women who arrived on the four ships were caught between two clashing ideologies: the Anglican missionaries who represented a patronizing institution that demanded obedience and compliance and the Female Middle-Class Emigration Society, an early English feminist organization, which aimed to send independent, educated women to the frontier.

The story of British Columbia's bride-ships is more complicated than the one started in France. The novelist and social critic Charles Dickens plays a major role, as does the richest woman in all England. The story is shaped, too, by elevated debate in the London *Times,* in letters penned to the press from the parlours of leading 19th-century English feminists such as Maria Rye and Bessie Parkes. Gentlemen travellers, officers of the Royal Navy, hardened frontier journalists, diarists and the sharpened voices of the colonial governing class all have their say. And all the while, like the mournful air of an Irish lament, one hears the muted voices of many displaced young women.

Here, then, are the women of British Columbia's bride-ships, the context of the times which set them on their way, their passage across cruel oceans and their work, liaisons and marriages. These are extraordinary stories of ordinary human beings who made profound contributions to the world of 1862, and thence to our own time. The adventures of these women, the angst they suffered and the success they achieved make a tale of truly epic proportions. Like Milton's Satan, theirs is a pilgrimage through chaos; their stories, taken together, are symbolic of the larger human condition.

Chapter One
LIBERALISM AND SQUALOR:
LONDON IN QUEEN VICTORIA'S HEYDAY

I stretch lame hands of faith and grope
And gather dust and chaff, and call
To what I feel is Lord of all
And faintly trust the larger hope.[1]

The moment had finally come. Florence Wilson had marked off each long day with a pencil on a plank of boxwood beneath her berth. At night she would lie on her straw mattress, listening to the constant, fearsome thundering of the ship and run her fingers over the ever-increasing number of small grooves. Florence wondered often if she or the *Tynemouth* would survive the voyage. She believed that it was only by God's mercy that they both had. Even now, warmed by the afternoon sun and assured by the soft green hills that closed around the inlet, she remembered the horror of that voyage.

"It's been 106 long days, Sophie, if you count the last two at anchor."

"I've counted every dreadful minute," Sophia Shaw retorted, "and I'll not stop counting until my feet touch land again. Flo, it's over, can you believe it? We are actually going *ashore*."

They laughed, clapped and jumped about on deck. They were now on board a Royal Navy gunboat, HMS *Forward,* steaming up Victoria's inner harbour. The magical word "ashore" was moments away. Sophia looked back at the *Tynemouth* only once. Beside them at the rail, jostling, pointing, chattering, were 57 other single women. Many were still in their adolescence; a few were older. All were full of excitement and apprehension.

"Just *look* at me, Aggie," Emily Morris was wailing to her sister. "An officer smiled at *me* and called *me* ma'am. He even touched his cap." She ran her hand through the mess of her tangled hair and over the blotched and grimy calico skirt. Tears were streaming.

"You're beautiful, Emily, and he knew it. Just wait till we get you a new dress and a proper wash." Emily, Augusta knew, was the quintessential English beauty, fine-boned, pale and thin, and would have no trouble with men. She darkened suddenly over the thought that sooner or later they would part.

On shore, hundreds of men were beginning to gather around the wharf at the end of the bay where the women would land. A cheer went up as the *Forward* rounded up, dropped anchor and slung out a longboat level with the rail.

"Aggie, I'm scared," Emily fretted.

"Don't be silly."

Shipbound for three and a half months, the women had been forbidden even short breaks ashore in the Falklands or San Francisco. The chaperones on board had also refused them any contact with the other passengers. Now they were literally surrounded by brawny young sailors in uniform, while a few hundred yards away a growing throng of virile locals clamoured eagerly for them to land.

"Come on then, ladies, in you go."

A naval rating, white shirt gleaming in the sun, held out his arm in a gesture of assistance. Many of the girls began to cry and hug each other. Two officers turned away and looked at the growing commotion on shore. The longboat remained empty until the chaperones, Reverend Scott and Mrs. Robb, stepped forward. Scott was dressed in the black suit of the Anglican missionary and carried a bible. Mrs. Robb wore a crisp black dress and a black shawl that covered her head. She gave one black-gloved hand to the rating and carried an ebony cane in the other. Moving gingerly to the front of the tender, she sat down, turned and ordered abruptly, "Girls, get in!"

Slowly the longboat filled. The older women hung back on deck and muttered under their breath, while the younger ones dutifully clambered over the wooden seats and sat down. Mr. Scott and Mrs. Robb sat by themselves.

As the longboat pulled away with the chaperones and its first load of anxious women, those remaining on the gunboat grew bolder. Some sang. Sophia cracked a rude joke. Florence laughed and pointed a finger at a blushing young officer. Emily bit the dirt out from under her nails.

Farther down the rail Jane Saunders and Clara Duren stood side by side, watching the crowd press forward as the girls were landed. The minister and the matron were shaking hands with well-dressed dignitaries. Suddenly one of the girls tripped and fell and a collective "Oh" went up from the crowd. She was helped up and the long line of uncertain immigrants began to move slowly up a corridor that divided the crowd.

"Clara, I'm terrified, aren't you?"

"No, I'm not, and you shouldn't be either," Clara asserted. "There are men here, good men, men who don't give a tinker's damn for our past lives or our social standing. They are honest, hard-working men who want good wives. You will marry and have fine children and a real home." Then the tone of her voice changed. "Something Lizzie will never have."

"Yes, God bless dearest Elizabeth," said Jane, sobered. "She should have been here."

"Well, at least it wasn't smallpox. Here, look at this." Clara was thinking of the stories Dr. Chipp, the *Tynemouth*'s surgeon, had told her about whole emigrant ships being wiped out by smallpox. She gave Jane a folded newspaper. "Dr. Chipp got it from the customs officer two nights ago. He gave it to me as a keepsake. They call us the women of the bride-ships."

Jane glanced at the headline about the arrival of the *Tynemouth*. "When you were helping Dr. Chipp with Elizabeth, Clara, did you like him?"

Clara didn't answer.

The longboat returned and filled again. Sophia and Florence were still laughing mischievously as they and the others clambered aboard. Emily smiled at the midshipman whose hand on the tiller guided the boat and the oarsmen the few hundred yards to shore. Clara noticed that Mary MacDonald, seated next to her, was shaking. As the boat neared the wharf, the crowd once again broke into raucous cheers. Caps and dust filled the air.

"Mary, my poor love, what's the matter, girl?" Clara hugged Mary tightly.

Mary sobbed uncontrollably. "I want to go home."

Seven months before, in London, Eden Colville, Esq., was feeling quite proud of himself. He was sitting in the lobby of one of the most famous and exclusive clubs in the city. Through industry and calculation he had recently become a respected member of the upper middle class. Still in his 40s, Eden was already a director of the Royal Mail Steam Packet Company and involved in business interests with the newly inaugurated Panama Railway. It was through that venture that he had travelled to America and while there made several trips north to the western plains. He had visited Hudson's Bay Company outposts on both sides of the 49th parallel and had much to say to company factors about the efficient transportation of furs to England. At home, he had gained the attention of Hudson's Bay Company officials in London, so much so that he had been asked to represent the "Honourable Company" at the important meeting at the club that evening.

Confident, politically astute and a staunch Anglican, Eden nodded at the servant who brought him a brandy and turned to the financial pages of the *Times* of London. Though not completely accepted by members of the peerage, he was fast becoming a member of the gentry. Eden certainly felt that he had arrived.

It was the rainy, late afternoon of Thursday, February 27, 1862, and Eden had come to The London Tavern in the middle of Bishops Gate Street to hear a report that interested him. Waiting for the meeting to begin, Eden wondered about what he might have to say. Restless and alert, he admired the Georgian architecture. Directly in front of him, just beyond the lobby, was the famous Pillar Room. Here, tall Corinthian columns and pilasters separated large paintings by William Powell Frith and Ford Madox Brown. To the left was the celebrated Surrey Oak dining room. Eden wandered over and perused the menu posted in front of two large doors that were carved with the image of Britannia striding the waves.

The chef's specialty that evening was turtle cutlets and turtle soup. The turtles themselves were kept in a large tank in one of the cool vaults in the cellar along with barrels of porter, pipes of port, butts of sherry and thousands of bottles of claret, champagne and other wine. The turtles would survive in this cool, aquamarine memory of the Pacific for up to three months, provided the water in which they had been brought to England was not changed. Eden smiled to himself; at least *here*, the chef would know *that*.

Eden stepped back and looked up. Two floors above the lobby he could just see the Venetian-glass doors of the ballroom. It extended the whole length of the building and often doubled as a banquet hall for over 300 male members. It had seats for 150 ladies who, of course, were admitted only as spectators in the galleries at each end.

The London Tavern had stood on this spot since 1768. Eden mused on that fact and considered with some vanity just how far he had come. A gentleman rushed by, late for a meeting of the Mexican Bondholders on the second floor. Settling down again with the *Times,* Eden read in the shipping news that the tea clipper *Kate Carnie* had arrived in London on February 20, 113 days out from Shanghai. This was, he knew, good news for the tea brokers in Mincing Lane. Then a porter gently reminded him that his meeting was about to begin. Folding the paper, Eden rose, walked up to the salon on the mezzanine and took a chair near the back.

The occasion was a meeting of the Columbia Mission Society, a charitable organization affiliated with the Church of England. Its purpose was to secure Anglican missionaries for the British colonies of Vancouver Island and the mainland on the faraway west coast of British North America. The society was just two years old and had already attracted a lot of attention. The special invitation had been delivered personally to "E. Colville, Esq." at his office by a young boy who deferentially took off his cap. It suggested that this meeting was to be very important. Looking about the room Eden noticed members of the House of Commons, Anglican bishops and other High Churchmen, senior members of the armed forces and influential friends of the Columbia Mission.

"Good Lord," he muttered. Eden recognized the Right Honourable William Corbitt, the Lord Mayor of London, and Arthur Kinnaird, M.P. The Lord Bishop of Oxford, the Very Reverend Samuel Wilberforce, was drinking tea and being very earnest with the Reverend Gleig, chaplain-general to the armed forces. Sir Harold Verney, M.P., was talking loudly with Mr. Abel-Smith, a director of the West India Mail Packet Company. Eden overheard that Sir Harold's eldest son, Edmund, had just been posted to Vancouver Island as commander of HMS *Grappler*. Archibald Campbell Tait, the Bishop of London, was pressing a point with a Captain Petrie; Eden wasn't sure, but he knew he was something-or-other in the army. The Reverend John Garrett, deputy secretary to the Columbia Mission, held a gavel and shuffled papers. The tall, refined gentleman standing off to one side was the newly consecrated Lord Bishop of Honolulu, the Reverend Nettleship Staley.

Eden also saw the Countess of Falmouth, Mrs. Tait and Mrs. Corbitt seated at the front. Sitting beside them was Miss Angela Burdett Coutts, noted philanthropist and heir to the Coutts Bank fortune. Eden strained to see if Charles Dickens, the novelist and close friend of Miss Burdett Coutts, was with her. He had heard that their relationship was more than just amiable, but Dickens was not present.

Suddenly Garrett straightened up and struck his gavel, and the smoky room came to order. All was quiet as the Reverend T. J. Rowsell gave the prayer. Then the Lord Mayor rose and said:

Ladies and Gentlemen, I need hardly tell you what the object of our meeting today is. You are well aware of the nature of the good work in which we are called upon to participate. Nothing can partake more of the nature of true philanthropy than helping to give Religious consolation to those of our fellow-countrymen who are encountering perils in the wild and distant parts of the world, subduing the earth and fighting the great battle of life. To such people Religious support must be one of vital necessity; and we, the English people, whose mission it is, I think, to Christianize the world — must acknowledge that it is our duty, as far as we possibly can, to aid in such a work. [Hear, hear.] I am very happy to have the privilege of prevailing on this occasion. [Cheers.][2]

His Lordship then called upon Garrett to explain the history of the society to new members. Garrett, who was also vicar of St. Paul's near Penzance, Cornwall, had already slowed his speech like that of his west country parishioners, but he now, purposefully, adopted a very Oxford accent. He carefully outlined the philanthropic beginnings of the Columbia Mission Society, noting that it was "founded under the spiritual promptings of a nobly generous heart." He raised his arm in the direction of its benefactor, Angela Burdett Coutts, and continued, "and further supported by a generous grant from Queen Victoria."[3] Miss Burdett Coutts nodded once to the assembly; everyone applauded.

Garrett then described the work of the missionaries currently in the Sandwich Islands. As he mentioned British Columbia he cleared his throat and raised his voice. He began to speak of his younger brother Alexander, a newly ordained missionary who had found himself stopping over in the Sandwich Islands for a month en

8

route to British Columbia.[4] Garrett explained that his brother had had great success converting the islanders and had even suggested that a bishopric be established in Honolulu, to which the church had quickly agreed. Everyone applauded again.

When Garrett read an excerpt from his brother's letter, giving details of his current missionary life among the Saanich Indians, north of Victoria on Vancouver Island, the interest of the crowd sharpened, for this place was the focus of the meeting. Garrett began by reading about female domestics in the colonies:

> It is quite useless, and a waste of money and law, to
> engage female servants in England, at twenty pounds a year,
> and bind them to remain with employers here [Columbia]
> for five years. The moment such a servant lands here, she
> can obtain without one hour's delay, sixty, seventy, and even
> eighty pounds per annum wages, together with innumerable
> offers and promises of marriage.[5]

A buzz of conversation swept the room. Interest was further piqued when Garrett again cleared his throat and held up another letter. "I have seldom read a missionary letter of more practical interest and value than this letter from Mr. Brown, and I hope your lordship will think a few sentences deserve to be used here."[6] He was referring to the Reverend R. C. Lundin Brown, who, while ministering to the prospectors in a strange-sounding place called Lillooet, was appalled by the number of illicit relationships the miners conducted with both native and white women. Like all Anglican missionaries, Brown believed that frontier prostitution would "ultimately ruin Religion and morals in this fine country."[7] Garrett then continued to read from Brown's letter:

Dozens of men have told me they would gladly marry if they could. I was speaking one evening on the subject of the dearth of females, and mentioned my intention of writing to beg that a plan of emigration be set on foot; whereupon one member of the company immediately exclaimed, "Then, sir, I pre-empt a wife;" another, and another, and all round the circle of those listening to me earnestly exclaimed the same.[8]

Picking up on the crowd's buzzing interest, Garrett read more theatrically:

Fancy the idea of pre-empting a wife! Yet, I assure you, this touches at the root of the greatest blessing which can now be conferred upon this Colony from home.
Think of the 600,000 more women at home than there are men, and then think what society must be here. Churches may and must be built, our faithful witness must be born for holiness and virtue, but where there is no wedded life, church-going must be difficult because morality is almost impossible.[9]

Garrett told the assembly that the earnest and practical young missionary in Lillooet had already written to the shipping agents in London who had served the Columbia Mission Society in the past. Brown persuaded them to allow free baggage for the women who might go out. He had also convinced Drummond and Masterman's Bank that they should set up an emigration fund account to raise money for fares. A mutter of approval swept the room. Building upon the optimism, Garrett asserted that Brown had already corresponded with Arthur Kinnaird, M.P., and had persuaded him to act as the treasurer should such a fund come to pass. Mr. Kinnaird stood up, looked about, waved and sat down. There was much applause.

Brown was betting on Garrett's enthusiasm to prompt a motion calling for the establishment of a society whose mandate would be to find and supply good Christian women for this new colonial venture. Garrett's spirited eloquence worked. Kinnaird was on his feet again, speaking at length of the value of the Columbia Mission Society and its work in the colonies. When he finally recommended adopting a plan to sponsor single women to the mainland colony under the name of the Columbia Emigration Society, Eden saw his opportunity. He stood up, cleared his throat and seconded the motion; applause broke out spontaneously. When Miss Burdett Coutts offered to back the motion to the tune of £15,000 she was given a standing ovation.

Then speaker after speaker rose to express support; each, it seemed, tried to outdo the other. When a more cautious gentleman wondered if the Hudson's Bay Company would resist the idea of encouraging settlement on land over which it held a trading monopoly, Abel-Smith rose and put the momentary fears to rest. He stated with confidence that several Hudson's Bay Company directors in London were his close friends, and he was sure that the company would offer its complete co-operation. The pronouncement was greeted with more wild applause. Suddenly, others were on their feet clamouring to be heard. Eden was thrilled by the excitement of it all. He felt that history was in the making and that he had, at last, become part of it.

When Reverend Wilberforce stood up to give his opinion, others deferred. With authority he began. "Consider the number, for instance, of young girls brought up in the union workhouses of this country. You know that these young girls, having no future before them as they pass from girlhood into early womanhood, come into perpetual contact with the worst of their own sex, whose miseries bring them back to the workhouse. [Hear, hear.]" Then Wilberforce, an old hand at oratory, drove home the point that it was the mission society's duty to save these lost souls. Eden listened intently and it seemed that the bishop was addressing him directly. "You will have made homes in that distant land, you will have made morality possible, you will have made Christian homes a fact, you will have made the elevating influences of women's society a healing blessing to those adventurous souls. [Cheers.]"[10] Eden, arms folded across his chest, nodded and said to the gentleman seated next to him that the motion was in the bag. Suddenly, near the front, a young man was on his feet. With a rolled newspaper in his outstretched arm, he demanded loudly that the question should be put. The rest of the evening was a blur.

Outside, Eden waited for a hansom cab. It had stopped raining, but the night was foggy and cold. He filled his lungs with the dank air. Several members patted him on the shoulder as they passed; one shook his hand and exclaimed, "Well done, Eden," and walked on. Alone, he thought about the Bishop of Honolulu's closing prayer. He loved the phrase "a new Jerusalem" that the bishop had used, because it reminded him of his favourite hymn.

Eden was tired but energized by the evening and knew that Abel-Smith would tell the Hudson's Bay Company directors that he had seconded the motion. They would understand and appreciate the politics of his timely initiative. He smiled, thinking out loud, "How far England has come since the Exhibition! How humanitarian, how Christian!"

Eden was proud of himself, both as a businessman and as a Christian. He had observed how life in England, from its national politics to its foreign policy, had, in the past ten years, become simply an extension of the Anglican Church, and that evening he had taken part in the collaboration. Yet — and perhaps it was the weather for the rain had started again — Eden had a nagging doubt: the unemployment, the poor, the workhouses.

"Why," he wondered, "must hundreds of thousands of England's people still be forced to leave our shores each year?"

Queen Victoria's heyday, the decade between 1851 and 1861, was, for Eden Colville and others like him, a time of wealth. When the queen and her beloved consort, Prince Albert, opened the Great Exhibition in London's Hyde Park on May 1, 1851, they set off a decade of progress and prosperity that made England the envy of the world. Rapid developments in industry had made the country a pioneer of modernity, while successive governments had created a new liberalism and a humanitarian spirit. The firm hand of the colonial office oversaw British rule in Africa, India, Australia, North America and the Pacific. The sun never set on the British Empire or, at least, so it appeared.

For the merchant class, the railways, the icon of the age of steam, turned ports like Ramsgate, Hastings and Brighton into their personal playgrounds. Soon, railway expansion and amalgamations gave every English hamlet its own thriving station. The screw propeller resulted in the new iron steamships which were faster and safer than side-wheelers, and shipbuilding and the production of steel created a boom along the River Tyne. In the Midlands, the mills were mechanized and the export of cotton and other goods from Liverpool rivalled that from London. The need for coal to fuel all these belching boilers brought prosperity to Cardiff, Newcastle and hundreds of smaller towns in the coal belt.

By the 1850s, even conditions for the working poor were slowly improving. England's "dark, satanic mills" were being inspected, albeit sporadically, and the Factory Acts forbade children under nine from working. Women and juveniles ten years old and over could work, but were limited to a ten-hour day. The men who laboured in the foundries and coke plants worked much longer, however, and the wretched cough of consumption was still heard throughout the land. Some reformers like the Lever Brothers, the soap makers, were moved to provide better housing. As faceless and claustrophobic as the new boroughs of row housing were, they were, at the time, a marked improvement over the slums from which the poor had originally come. It would take only 20 years for the proliferation of such "towns" to turn England's "green and pleasant land"[11] into a wilderness of dirty brick.

The reforms were, for many, too little, too late. Eden Colville's anxieties were right: there *was* a Janus-faced quality to this time. While mechanization had done much to raise the standard of living, overproduction and speculation had created inevitable cycles of growth and depression. Eden recalled the earlier stories of privation that he had heard from his mother.

In 1836, Stockport had been hit by a depression, and wages fell from seven shillings a week to one. Soon, a quarter of all the houses were empty. By year's end, one fifth of the population of Birmingham was on relief. He thought back to the stories his grandmother had told him of life in the village of Swaffham when a ha'penny herring was divided among four people and the burnt stale crusts of bread were ground up and added to the precious leaves of tea. "Crammings," he remembered, was the sluice made from chaff, water and flour that was normally fed to pigs; it had been, for a time, his grandmother's daily fare. If a man was caught stealing a sheep or poaching a pheasant to avoid starvation, he was sent to Van Dieman's Land for 14 years.

By 1845, over 300,000 desperate young men had fled to the colonies. Hundreds of old sailing hulks that barely floated became emigrant ships. Thousands of people departed virtually penniless after toiling for over a year just to raise the 30 shillings for a place in steerage. Many others stole simply to *be* deported. By the 1850s, England was hemorrhaging; the best of its young men were gone and the women were left behind. The census of 1861 revealed that in England and Wales alone, there was an "excess" of 209,663 women between the ages of 20 and 25.

The opportunities that Eden had enjoyed were the result of changes made in the country's educational system that benefitted his gender alone. By the 1840s, the growing merchant class had rejected the public and grammar schools for their sons, largely because the boys were taught subjects considered irrelevant to the commerce that created their fathers' wealth. In consequence, the new entrepreneurs had built their own profit-making private schools, which taught business arithmetic as well as Homer. Charles Dickens went to one of these new schools in 1824, and because of it he was able to rise above the squalid slums of his boyhood. His short stay at Wellington House Academy was enough to spark a lifelong interest in providing educational opportunities for the other street urchins, like Fagin, whom he had once befriended in Warren's Blacking Factory, in the London of his youth.

It was, however, daughters of all classes who fared the worst. Initially, education for young women occurred only in the home; the parlour was their classroom. Among the poorer classes, girls with initiative and without a parlour were considered lucky if they found work operating the looms in the cotton mills. For the vast majority without access to the mills and lacking any formal schooling, the future offered only domestic service, the workhouse or prostitution. In upper-class homes a mother's tutelage was replaced by a private governess, who instructed obedient young women in languages, music, drawing and sewing. For many, marriage within their class was the only desired future. The young ladies of the upper class who wished to work found themselves untrained and unfit for the new commerce. They faced only menial, poor-paying jobs in printing houses or hairdressing, and governesses were two-a-penny. Without support from "papa," it was impossible for them to continue to live as they had. Unmarried, these women were forced to stay at home bearing the stigma of an entirely new label, the "distressed gentlewomen."

Middle-class young ladies began to attend female boarding schools only in the 1840s. Mary Ann Evans (George Eliot) attended Coventry Boarding School, where 18th-century manners were forced onto 19th-century morality and respectability. Mary rebelled and wrote of the heartache of loveless marriages in novels such as *Adam Bede,* in 1859, and *Silas Marner,* 1861. In an age of Christian charity and uncompromising religious conformity, the outlook for working girls and educated gentlewomen alike was bleak.

Since the beginning of the 19th century, the English parliament had consolidated wealth in the middle and upper classes, and in so doing had diminished the lives of women and the poor. Two acts of parliament were responsible. First, the Corn Laws subsidized English landowners who grew wheat (corn) when the supply was cut off during the Napoleonic Wars. When the wars ended in 1815, the Corn Laws prevented the removal of the subsidy. The rich profited and the poor continued to pay for bread that was artificially overpriced for the next 30 years.

To quell the growing unrest, upper-class parliamentarians then created the Poor Laws in 1834. These laws demonized the indigent by claiming they took advantage of relief. Rationalized by parliament as a means of restoring the dignity of the poor labourer who had come to depend on the dole, the Poor Laws cut the heart out of a system of relief that had worked for centuries. Simply, the old allowance system, which had been administered by local communities, was scrapped; instead, poor people were entitled to relief only if they entered the workhouse. The aid given through the humane, medieval parish was centralized and the compassion of the church, which was responsible for finding work for the unemployed, was replaced with the severity of the workhouse. The workhouse was made not only a condition of welfare, but an actual deterrent to it: conditions in them were worse than the worst-case scenario of any labourer earning his own livelihood. Life in the workhouse became so intolerable that many soon chose the street. Women too gaunt for prostitution were without hope:

> She had sewn in the breast of her gown, the money to pay for her burial. If she could wear it through the day, and then lie down to die under the cover of darkness, she would be independent. If she were captured, the money would be taken from her as a pauper who had no right to it, and she would be carried to the accursed workhouse.[12]

Children were treated the most brutally, but single women, the aged and the chronically ill suffered terribly when they were incarcerated in the workhouse.

Poverty in the Victorian Age had become a moral issue. There were the "deserving poor," who worked hard, worshipped regularly and paid due deference to the class above; they were expected to take every indignity that was hurled at them with stoicism. The others, the undeserving poor, were the convicts, revolutionaries and undesirables. They were seen to undermine political stability and to be a threat to the very idea of progress. Progress was the paradigm, and it soon became attached to notions of Christian evangelism: to be industrious was an expression of faith; to be unemployed was to be cast in with the devil. Those who *did* more, *were* more, in Christian terms. Those who did less, the poor, were the corrupted, and hence they could be dismissed.

Most people came to believe that sending the poor overseas would give workers at home another chance, and at the same time rid England of its undesirables. It was in the interests of the British economy to subsidize an emigrant's passage abroad, as the country's growing population was felt to be a drain on the wealth of the nation. A few, like Thomas Carlyle, did speak out against the injustices of *laissez-faire* capitalism, but these humanitarian voices were largely drowned out. An official emigration policy, it was suggested, would also serve Britain's imperialist aims in North America: American President Polk's election slogan of "Manifest Destiny" could be countered by sending out emigrants to settle the empty land north of the 49th parallel in order to keep it for the empire. Yet the cry for action among the privileged classes was, in reality, little more than a self-serving anthem extolling the benefits of shovelling out the poor.

In 1837, parliament created an Agent-General for Emigration. In 1838, the British American Land Company began to assist Scottish Highlanders to go to the Maritimes and in 1840, the Colonial Secretary received an annual parliamentary grant of £1,500 to assist emigrants bound for Upper Canada. New Zealand and Australia adopted similar programs for immigrants arriving on their shores. Everywhere and in every class, emigration was seen to be the solution to deeply rooted social and economic problems. Soon, government-sponsored emigration societies mushroomed in all parts of the land, from Penzance in Cornwall to Stornoway in the Hebrides.

When Eden read that the American Civil War had significantly reduced the quantity of raw cotton reaching the mill towns, he knew it was only a matter of time before the populations of whole towns in the industrial north would once again be thrown out of work. He was right. Government intervention was slow and by the end of 1862, the exodus of politically disgruntled and socially embittered citizens out of England had reached a total of 500,000. Private philanthropic societies filled the vacuum created by the withdrawal of government funding, though most helped only young men to emigrate. Eden Colville, Angela Burdett Coutts and others of the Columbia Mission Society turned their attention to the women.

Heiress to her grandfather's Coutts Bank millions, Angela Georgina Burdett Coutts was the typical Victorian upper-class lady of good breeding. She was tall, thin, plain, reserved and intelligent. She was a product of the religious revivalism of the 1830s and her simple fundamentalism was tempered by a keenly developed sense of *noblesse oblige*. Distressed by her father's early death, she had, at 24, decided to dedicate her life and her fortune to philanthropy.

Angela Burdett Coutts met Charles Dickens in 1838 when he was a dashing, urbane young gentleman of 27. Nonconformist and brash, he had long, curly, brown hair and shining eyes. *The Pickwick Papers* and *Oliver Twist* had already made him famous. Within a year Dickens and Burdett Coutts had become the best of friends. She gained a trusted advisor and administrator of her charitable work in him, and a surrogate son in his oldest son, Charley. From her, he gained emotional support for his controversial public readings and intellectual support for his views on social reform. Together, they forged a bond of mutual concern that would change the lives of many of London's poor forever.

In 1834, Dickens, remembering his impoverished youth, began to fund the Ragged Schools, schools meant for the street urchins too wretched to be accepted at other charity schools. The Ragged Schools offered the incentive of at least temporary release from the brutal life in the factories that had trapped so many of Dickens's boyhood contemporaries. Dickens wrote of them in *Oliver Twist*.

More, Dickens and Burdett Coutts planned and built Columbia Square, a housing complex for working families in East London, a sewing school and soup kitchens for destitute seamstresses in Spittlefields, and a co-educational school in St. Stephens, Westminster. When Burdett Coutts turned her attention to London's prostitutes, Dickens provided her with a relevant educational curriculum. She used many of his ideas in Urania Cottage, her new home for "fallen" women.

It was Dickens who first suggested to Burdett Coutts the idea of female emigration. He wrote to her wondering "whether the Government would assist you to the extent of informing you from time to time into what distant parts of the World women could be sent for marriage."[13] It was not just serendipitous that Burdett Coutts should have been present at the London Tavern meeting of the Columbia Mission Society to hear Reverend Brown's letter from Lillooet. She had endowed the society in 1859, and funded the bishopric of British Columbia, enabling George Hills, the bishop, and his pastors, John Sheepshanks and Lundin Brown among them, to bring the Anglican Church to the mining camps of Canada's most westerly mainland colony. Dickens's prompt and Brown's plea had come together, the Columbia Emigration Society had found a ready sponsor and a bold new plan was born.

Charles Dickens called his friendship with Angela Burdett Coutts "intimate." He dedicated his sixth novel, *Martin Chuzzlewit,* to her, and spoke openly to her of his despair over his marriage. They were not lovers, yet they remained the perfect 19th-century couple, driven and outer-directed. They were equally energetic, both had suffered the demoralizing impact of youthful loss and were full of the evangelical fire of the Victorian bourgeoisie.

Strangely, Angela Burdett Coutts had fallen in love with the arch-conservative Sir Arthur Wellesley. As an M.P., he had fought violently against any social reforms that would diminish the power of the upper class. Yet Wellesley was also a national hero and, as the Duke of Wellington, had saved Britain from France at Waterloo in 1815. Burdett Coutts proposed to him on February 7, 1847. He was 78; she was 33. He refused, but rumour had it they were married in secret anyway.

When Eden Colville helped create the Columbia Emigration Society, he probably was not thinking only of the good of England. More likely, he was thinking about his own daughters. Their future expectations were tied directly to the fact that they were decidedly *not* poor, but still very single. Philanthropy and Christian charity had addressed the problem of the dispossessed, but not solved it. Eden was upper middle class and still he worried. The newspapers of the day reported that there was a pronounced rise in Britain in the ratio of women to men, and Eden remembered that he had heard Reverend Garrett at the Columbia Mission meeting pronounce that there were "600,000 more women at home than there were men."[14] Eden knew his daughters' futures were limited, especially if they remained unmarried.

In his anxieties Eden was not alone. In late 1861, Barbara Bodichon, Bessie Parkes and other London feminists began to organize for upper-class women who were concerned about the limited employment opportunities for single, middle-class women. These "Ladies of Langham Place" created the Society For The Employment of Women and tried to initiate wider social acceptance of educated, working women by offering them jobs in male-dominated professions such as law-copying, editing and telegraphy, through their own office. The Ladies of Langham Place knew, however, that they could not accomplish much, and it was not long before they began to see emigration as a viable option for the women of this class.

"What shall we do with our old maids?" was the cry that had energized the fledgling women's movement in England throughout the late 1850s. Increasingly, London feminists demanded that the government should provide work for middle-class young ladies who wished to remain in England. Others extolled the virtue of sending single, educated gentlewomen abroad, alone. This latter idea was far more shocking, and was met with lively debate from within feminist circles at exactly the same time as the Columbia Mission announced its new emigration society.

The feminist Bessie Parkes had founded *The English Women's Journal* in 1858; through it she articulated the views that were current amongst bluestockings. Bessie had faith that life in the colonies for all women would be far less tedious than long hours sitting in print shops or worse, before an officious misogynist, in some Dickensian law office:

> Seeing, as I do daily, how great is the comparative delicacy both in brain and in the bodily frames of women of the middle and upper class, of the bad effect on them of long hours of sedentary toil, the more anxious I become to see the immense surplus of the sex in England lightened by judicious, well conducted, and morally guarded emigration to our colonies, where the disproportion is equally enormous, and where they are wanted in every social capacity.[15]

Though she was perhaps naïve about the working conditions for *any* woman on a colonial frontier, Bessie's view soon garnered a substantial following.

But it was with the publication of Maria S. Rye's address before London's Social Sciences Congress in 1861 that the moral issues surrounding single women's emigration moved beyond feminist circles into the realm of public debate. Maria founded the Female Middle-Class Emigration Society in May 1862. "Are women to perish simply because they are women?" she cried. "Hundreds of educated women have been thrown upon their own resources, women of unblemished character, and, in many instances, women of capability and power."[16] The spirit of her address was spellbinding. She concluded by urging independent-minded women everywhere to address the strong, anti-feminist sentiment of the day:

> Teach your proteges to emigrate; send them where the men want wives, the mothers want governesses, where the shopkeepers, the schools, and the sick will thoroughly appreciate your exertions, and heartily welcome your women.[17]

Rye wanted her women working outside of the home; for many men of the time, that demand came as a shock.

Maria Rye led the debate in the *Times* by claiming that single women's emigration was already a foregone conclusion:

> Our work commenced last June; since then we have, at a cost of £800, sent out 33 governesses. I have also an impression, though all the colonies at present are scarcely prepared to assist me in a pecuniary manner, that the day is not far distant when a certain sum will be devoted to the introduction of women into our colonies of a class very superior to those now sent. A proposal to that effect is at present before the Melbourne Government, and I am very sanguine of its success.[18]

With the debate now in the press, Charles Kingsley, the well-known Christian Socialist, shot back. He argued that the emigration of professional working women would force women to compete with men, something he believed a woman was not meant to do. "All attempts to employ her in handicrafts are but substitutes for that far nobler and more useful work for which Nature intends her, to marry and bear children."[19] Despite Rye's efforts to find meaningful employment for single women abroad, Kingsley believed that the feminist plan would backfire, and soon become little more than a colonial marriage bureau. The issue of woman's emancipation from her traditional place in the Victorian family continued throughout all of April 1862.

Lord Osborne, conservative M.P., disagreed with Kingsley's assessment that single, middle-class women who emigrated to the colonies would become ravenous husband hunters. He thought middle-class women were entirely too coarse to make even adequate governesses. Feminists retorted with the notion that single women who ventured abroad were no more indelicate than "a girl who goes to a ball or archery meeting at home, and that marriage, after all, was a matter of choice, not geography."[20] Maria Rye continued to repeat that her goal was simply to find decent employment for women overseas.

The issue of female emigration had been seized upon by two groups, each with a special agenda. "Get them out," argued the males who believed that independent, single working women challenged historical notions of male superiority. The best place for the troublemakers, they felt, was abroad.

"Let's get out for a better life," argued the feminists who thought that middle-class women were ill-served in Britain, having to toil at tasks far too demeaning for their station. How the women's movement in London could believe that a woman's life on a colonial frontier would be any *less* indelicate than what was suffered at home, they didn't say.

Then the debate was fuelled further by the publication of the principles of the newly formed Columbia Emigration Society, which certainly did not embrace issues of women's liberation. In April 1862, the Reverend John Garrett, secretary of the Columbia Mission Society, wrote to the *Times,* clearly stating the position of the Church of England:

> Reliable information has reached this country, through various channels, of the inestimable value which a careful stream of emigration of industrious women from Great Britain would prove at the present stage in the rapid progress of the colony of British Columbia. It is an essential element in the sound growth of a new colony that the men who first open it out should be able to settle and surround themselves with the humanizing ties of family life.[21]

Clearly, the Anglican Church did not want a potentially disruptive, intellectual class of women on its frontier.

> First, we could not guarantee suitable homes on reaching the colony to women who should depend on brains alone for support. Nor does it seem desirable to withdraw [female] teachers in families and schools at home. Those who go out under the protection of this society will agree to take service.
> Secondly, it is not the wish of this society to unsettle or withdraw from their valuable duties the trained and efficient domestic servants who have good employment and ample remuneration for their services at home.[22]

The Columbia Emigration Society did not wish to sponsor "distressed gentlewomen" who might, once in the colonies, have notions of independence. It wanted unemployed lower-class females, first to enter domestic service abroad, and then to marry in the faith. For the overseeing Columbia Mission Society, the issue was not the improvement of an already privileged woman's position, but the rescue of young women who were forced to the streets. The Christian organization thought emigration would provide the friendless girls in the orphanages of London with a second chance. Like the Reverend Lundin Brown in Lillooet, the Columbia Mission Society was primarily in the business of saving lost souls. The souls the society was after were the unsavoury souls of the frontier miners. What the girls themselves wanted did not seem to matter.

The appearance of Reverend Garrett's letter was most timely, in that it forced the feminists to question their priorities. Maria Rye's London Female Middle-Class Emigration Society could either become an agency concerned only with placing ideologically enthusiastic feminists in the colonies, or it could remain a colonial employment agency, intent upon finding opportunities for *any* woman of the middle class who wished simply to work abroad. Both needed jobs, one came with a specific political agenda. Maria Rye had to consider whether her agency would sponsor the single females who would carry on the feminist cause in the colonies, or work to provide support largely for those displaced and disadvantaged at home. That decision, for the moment, was delayed, for by the middle of May 1862, Maria faced the immediate problem of organizing the emigration of a number of educated gentlewomen who had come forward, simply desiring a better life overseas.

The Female Middle-Class Emigration Society began, on its own, to investigate contacts in British Columbia that might be interested in helping these women find suitable placements when they arrived. The response from some influential members of the ruling elite in Victoria was daunting. Sarah Crease, wife of Attorney-General Henry Pellew Crease, wrote, "I regret that I cannot give you any hopes of being able to benefit educated women by sending them out here."[23] She, as others, believed Vancouver Island was no place for *any* single women, save a few necessary domestic servants. "The bane of the country," she continued, "is drink; assisted much by the removal of the pressure of that portion of public opinion consisting of social and family influence, which at home has so powerful an effect on keeping things straight."[24]

When Maria Rye read of the formation of the Columbia Emigration Society she wrote to the Columbia Mission Society in London asking if her clients might travel with the Columbia Mission girls. She received a most surprising answer. The newly formed Columbia Emigration Society needed an organizer of Maria Rye's calibre, and offered her instead the opportunity to oversee the whole operation. She accepted immediately.

Suddenly, things were abuzz. She first had to make contact with the directors of the Columbia Emigration Society; she had to meet with those women who were directly in her charge and she had to arrange for them immediate placement when they arrived in British Columbia. Beyond this, she had to contend with the daily operation of her own agency and respond to a growing body of women who wished information. More, all of these things had to be accomplished in a month.

Throughout all of this, Maria Rye thought about what she was doing. Could such a mix of street-wise, teenage female orphans and ladies of some breeding even live together on a sea voyage of at least half a year? The *Tynemouth,* the vessel that the Columbia

Emigration Society had already chartered for the mission, was going to be full. Maria Rye did not have the time to consider the suitability of the vessel, its captain or crew; in that, she simply hoped for the best. For Florence, Sophie, Emily, Aggie, Jane, Clara, Mary and a host of others, the great adventure was about to begin.

Chapter Two
VIOLENCE IN THE BLACK CANYONS:
THE MOIL FOR GOLD

This is the payday up at the mines, when the bearded
brutes come down;
There's money to burn in the streets tonight, so I've sent
my Klooch to town,
With a haggard face and a ribband of red entwined in her
hair of brown.

And I know at the dawn she'll come reeling home with
the bottles one, two, three
One for herself, to drown her shame, and two big bottles for me
To make me forget the thing that I am and the one I used to be.[1]

Had the Reverend Lundin Brown known what awaited
him in the black canyons, he might never have come.
As it was, he stayed only five years. For millennia, as
the whirling torrents cut deep canyons out of the black rock of the
coastal mountains, the Fraser River and its treasures had belonged

solely to the natives. The golden nuggets that lay atop the river bars from Cache Creek to Hope brought the men and then the missionaries. The seductive ore seemed there for the taking. The miners who lusted after it were as raw, as hard and as dark as the canyons themselves. In the beginning those who had long dwelt there were pushed off; those who resisted were shot.

Like a perverted Midas, the touch of gold soon became a curse; it defiled civility and community and replaced it with maniacal conceit. The lure of the beguiling metal affected the miners even before they reached the river. It smote them on the diggings and haunted them when they left. A year after his arrival, the Reverend Brown's plan to bring good Christian women for the miners seemed to him the last ray of hope. The violence he saw was as overwhelming as the land was large, and it made him sick.

In mid-August 1858, displaced natives sent the corpses of ten decapitated miners down the Fraser River. At Fort Yale, prospectors heading upstream stood by horrified as the bodies were pulled from the slowing silt. Days later at nearby Deadman's Bend, 19 more beheaded miners were seen floating in an eddy. By week's end, at Fort Hope, the river gave up 32 miners' remains. Many of the bodies, it was said, had been disfigured. That same month Kent and Smith's Express Company reported that Indians had attacked and killed two French miners as they were digging at Big Canyon. The violence, it seemed, was everywhere. The *Victoria Gazette* had already reported a rumour that 2,000 Indians were assembled and ready for war just 15 miles above Fort Yale. When news reached Victoria of the murder of 22 barricaded miners by Couteau (Knife) Indians up the Fraser Canyon, the call for blood began. Without a police force, order in the black canyons soon descended to the way of the vigilante. Without the rule of law, there would be only the mentality of the mob.

Governor James Douglas of Vancouver Island was well aware of the flood of miners to the goldfields. In an attempt to control the growing numbers and mindful of the American notion of Manifest Destiny, he issued a proclamation for an area over which he had no jurisdiction. He decreed that all the gold found on the mainland was the property of the British Crown. More, the governor demanded that each prospector buy a mining licence at ten shillings per head per month, in order to work the bars on the Fraser River. He marked the common crossing spots along the 49th parallel as entry points into British territory and forbade American vessels that were carrying guns, liquor and ammunition to enter the Fraser. He then dispatched the Royal Navy gunboat, HMS *Satellite,* to Sandheads at the mouth of the river, to act as enforcer.

Many officials in Britain praised Douglas's actions, but a few did not. Sir Edward Bulwer Lytton, the British Colonial Secretary, was convinced that Douglas, as a former Hudson's Bay Company chief factor, had resisted the settlement of Vancouver Island. Bulwer Lytton knew that Douglas had opposed Britain's policy of Free Trade and felt that he simply did not wish to forward the gold taxes to London. In July 1858, Bulwer Lytton introduced a bill in the British Parliament making the mainland a new Crown colony, responsible to Westminster.

As administrator of the new region, Governor Douglas was, ironically, instrumental in creating the violence in the goldfields that he sought to curtail. Initially, there were two routes to the fur-bearing regions up-country. One was the direct and dangerous route up the Fraser River itself, where packhorses and men often fell from a makeshift trail that was carved, and sometimes hung, from the sheer canyon walls. The other, favoured by Douglas when he was chief factor, bypassed the treacherous ravines altogether. It was a more roundabout route up the Harrison River system to

Port Douglas at the end of Harrison Lake. Here, goods could be moved by river steamer in and out of the interior more safely and more cheaply than the precipitous canyon trail. With Douglas's blessing, Fort Yale, which stood at the start of the Fraser Canyon, was abandoned in 1849.

However, with a gold strike in March 1858 at Hill's Bar, a stone's throw from Fort Yale, the Harrison route was ignored. Rumours of riches drew thousands of hopefuls directly up the Fraser toward the derelict old fort. Despite the growing violence between natives and miners on the river's gravel bars, it did not take long for the wily governor to revive the garrison of decaying buildings. Late in 1858, he decreed Yale a township, issued liquor licences and sent a gold commissioner, and sat back to rake in the new taxes. The miners, driven by "Fraser River Fever" and fortified by the promise of readily available alcohol, soon swarmed up to Yale. Often, they arrived in a hail of bullets. Governor Douglas thought it enough to hire just two police constables. He couldn't have been more wrong.

The prospectors scoffed at any obstacle, be it local constables, the 49th parallel, or a thundering gorge of the Fraser River. Well supplied with knives, guns, booze, American flags and bravado, they headed for British Columbia on foot, by home-built scow, or by any paddle-wheel steamer with deck space to take them. By mid-summer of 1858, some 30,000 miners had turned colonial Victoria from a very bucolic English backwater into a seething way-station of decidedly un-English aliens.

Lieutenant Charles Wilson, secretary to the British Boundary Commission, was there:

> You are hardly safe without arms & even with them, when
> you have to walk along paths across which gentlemen with a

brace of revolvers each are settling their differences; the whiz
of revolver bullets round you goes on all day & if anyone
gets shot of course it's his own fault; however I like the
excitement very much & never felt better in my life.[2]

Wilson may have felt good in Victoria, but he was definitely in
the minority. John Lord, a naturalist with the Boundary
Commission and friend of Charles Wilson, was also in Victoria
that first summer of the Fraser River gold rush. He captured the
more common feeling:

In all directions were canvas tents, from the white strip
stretched over a ridgepole, to the great canvas store. The
rattle of the dice-box, the droning invitation of the keepers
of the Monte-tables, the discordant sounds of badly-played
instruments, angry words, oaths too terrible to name,
roistering songs with noisy refrains, were all signs significant
of the golden talisman that met me on every side, as I
elbowed my way amidst the unkempt throng that were
waiting means of conveyance to take them to the auriferous
bars of the far-famed Fraser River.[3]

The lure of gold was only part of it; the miners were coming to
the great unknown. The unmapped high plateaus and mountain
ranges west of the Rockies were real enough, but they were also a
place of the mind: in the context of 19th-century Romanticism, a
visionary frontier. The mighty Fraser began in the sun and in the
blue and blinding seracs of unknown glaciers high in the empty
mountains of the central Rockies. The tangible reward for the
journey was certainly gold, though just as real for many was the
more intangible one; the quest for a place in the imagination.

Other than a few scattered Hudson's Bay Company outposts, the British Columbia interior was, for Europeans at least, a timeless, unnamed and untouched land. To be sure, it drew those who would get rich from its resources, but it also called the artists and wanderers such as Frederick Whymper and Edward Coleman. They understood the capacity of the landscape to inspire and they painted it as they thought it should be. At the time of the Fraser River gold rush, British Columbia was still a mythic landscape, and the scale of it staggered the imagination.

When the Reverend Lundin Brown arrived at Lillooet, the best he could do to place himself in this immensity for his English friends was to mark his spot in the northern vastness by compass co-ordinates:

> The position of Lillooet on the map is lat. 50°41'N, and close upon the 122nd parallel of west longitude. Beyond the town, the eye rests with pleasure on a series of terraces or benches, the fields enclosed and cultivated, blossoming and garden-like. Further still, yonder silvery line marks the winding of the river, until it disappears among the distant hills.[4]

At the confluence with the Thompson River, the lighter, more yellow slopes of the interior meet the canyons of the Fraser. Here the constricted waters begin their tumultuous roar down to the sea. This is a deadly place where deep in the gorges, standing waves, over-falls, eddies, whirlpools and cataracts mock the persistent salmon. Here, "the first explorers crawled on hands and knees along the edges of the precipice, where the Indians traveled on dangling ladders, where the gold rush hauled its freight by a road built on stilts."[5] In the canyons, even the convulsions of a current that snapped the trees and mangled the fish could not thwart the men besotted by gold.

It wasn't surprising that the violence on the river had begun in confrontations with the natives. Victoria was overrun, not only with miners from all over the globe who were heading for the goldfields, but also with aboriginals who travelled across the bridge from the Songhees reserve. Of the "heathen savages," the native males were felt to be a threat to Victoria's white women and their children, yet it was the native women who received the brunt of the prejudice. Amazingly, they were the ones blamed with corrupting the morality of the miners. The *British Colonist* intoned, "a dance house is only a hell hole where the females are white; but it is many times worse where they are squaws."[6] The ensuing prostitution, disorderly conduct and mixed-race relationships cut to the very heart of Victoria's civilized, Christian society. In response, Victoria's constabulary was known to shave the heads of aboriginal women who were charged with prostitution. In 1861, Victoria's council evicted Indians from the streets of the city altogether. The fear of smallpox, which was beginning to show up among them, gave sanction to the eviction order, and masked the horror of sexual miscegenation that lay at the core of the legislation. Observing such public treatment by sober, Christian-minded city fathers, the lawless, itinerant miners found it easy to dismiss entirely the aboriginals they encountered on the frontier.

Soon, the gravel beds of the Fraser River were crawling with white prospectors who took far more than the sparkling golden nuggets. Working the bars with rockers and sluice-boxes from dawn to dark drove many of them to sheer exhaustion and they took to plundering whatever food was available. They pillaged the weirs beside the sandbars, destroyed salmon-spawning grounds, ate the fish that were the source of winter food, stole what few native crops they found, shot Indian horses and, it was said, abused native women.

For the prospector, everything was there for the taking. That conviction, fostered by a belief in white racial superiority, was further enhanced by a sense of anarchy prevalent among many transient Americans on the still-unguarded frontier. The prevailing "civilized" opinion of the day had actually supported much of the lawlessness. Indians were considered Stone Age people: licentious savages and simple-minded hunters and gatherers, who had no rights to the land because they did not cultivate it, nor exploit it in the manner of the Europeans. In June 1869, the *British Columbian* still argued that:

> According to the strict rule of international law, territory occupied by a barbarous or wholly uncivilized people may be rightfully appropriated by a civilized or Christian nation.[7]

In this view, Christian and thug stood firmly side by side.

However, in the summer of 1858, when the news of the floating, decapitated corpses reached the miners who were working the sandbars upriver, disregard soon turned into self-preservation. No one slept without a rifle, loaded and handy, and each man would take his turn as sentry during the long night's cold vigil. On duty, each was careful to keep his back to the rock and his eyes on the river.

They had good reason to be wary. The Fraser River was heavy with gold. The natives knew it, and wanted their share, but they were being crowded out. In mid-August 1858, the *Victoria Gazette* revealed the extent of the wealth:

> 8 companies on Texas Bar are making from $15 to $40 per day to the hand.

14 companies on Hill's Bar are making from $16 to $30 per day to the hand.

Mr. George Barton, agent for Ballou's Express on Pike's Bar, took out $45 on the 9th day of this month.[8]

The Chinese, who flooded to the sandbars vacated by miners, were generally believed to be in league with the natives. At Bancroft, it was reported that the Chinese had sold ammunition to the Indians along the river, and some prospectors forcibly tried to keep the Chinese below Yale. Many were beaten; some were killed. Poll-tax legislation, though defeated when introduced against the Chinese in 1860, set the tone of more dire things to come.

The atmosphere became decidedly more ominous when, later in the summer of 1858, a well-known white woman, one of the few in the Rancheria region north of Yale, was brutally murdered by natives. The fact that ten aboriginals were also killed in that exchange seemed not to matter; the death of a European woman was an affront. Now, along the Fraser, miners and settlers alike clamoured for government protection. Some demanded revenge.

On August 24, the *Victoria Gazette* published a communiqué which the residents at Fort Hope had sent to James Douglas, the Governor of Vancouver Island:

> Decapitated, denuded corpses of unfortunate adventurers are daily picked up on the river, while reports have reached us of the progress of retaliatory measures on the part of the whites, involving the indiscriminate slaughter of every age and sex. It has been advisable to apprise your Excellency of the existing state of affairs, that your Excellency may inaugurate and enforce such a series of measures as will check the further effusion of blood.[9]

Enraged and in fear, many miners had given up their claims and retreated to the relative safety of Fort Hope.

In Yale things deteriorated. One miner was shot in the back for simply refusing to buy another a drink. The only medical man in town, Dr. Fifer, was shot dead by one of his patients. It wasn't malpractice, though it easily could have been; it was professional rivalry and a hired gun. The good Dr. Crain of Fort Hope wanted Fifer's business, and readily found a hit man. In October 1858, two prospectors, Isaac Miller and Henry Post, fought a shoot-out in town over a claim at nearby Madison Bar. Miller was killed. In another claim dispute, the gold miner Mathias Neil was indicted in Yale for the murder of William Hartwell. Hartwell's body had been discovered at the confluence of the Fraser and Thompson rivers. Herman Wallace was shot dead on Front Street after a Sunday night brawl, an affront to the citizens of Yale, and their observance of the Sabbath.

D.W. Higgins was in Yale from the beginning. He had arrived on the old stern-wheeler *Enterprise* in late July 1858. A transplanted Nova Scotian, Higgins had moved to California in 1856, and become editor of the *Morning Call* newspaper. Selling out his interests, he joined the rush to the Fraser River goldfields and arrived there just as the violence began. More a poet than a profiteer, Higgins had ink and not gold in his blood. He became the Yale agent for William Ballou's Pioneer Fraser Express Company and was party to all the comings and goings of life in the community. The violence he witnessed along the river affected Higgins deeply, and he became a life-long advocate of British law and order. Higgins left Yale for Victoria in 1861, and eventually became editor of the *British Colonist.* For Higgins, Yale in 1858 was a complete hellhole:

> In every saloon a three-card Monte table was in full swing, and the halls were crowded to suffocation. A worse set of

cut-throats and all-round scoundrels than those who flocked to Yale from all parts of the world never assembled anywhere. Decent people feared to go out after dark. Night assaults and robberies, varied by an occasional murder or daylight theft were common occurrences. Crime in every form stalked boldly through the streets unchecked and unpunished. The good element was numerically large; but it was dominated and terrorized by those whose trade it was to bully, beat, rob, and slay. Often men who had differences in California met at Yale and proceeded to fight it out on British soil by American methods.[10]

Shoot-outs and barroom brawls were as much a part of life in the canyons as was the threat of Indian attack, yet these were not the only kind of outrage. Richard Hicks, the first gold commissioner in Yale, acquired 50-year leases on the best properties in town and then charged the wintering miners exorbitant rents. As the weary and often indigent prospectors headed for other settlements for the winter, the price of food brought in on the packtrains rose with the demand.

Charles Major worked for a time on the claims. He called it quits after the first winter of absolute poverty. He wrote home from Fort Hope:

We have been making two, three, and four dollars per day, but it would not last more than two or three days; and so you would spend that before you would find more. A party arrived here yesterday from Alexander, and they are a pitiful looking lot. When they got down here they had no shoes to their feet. Some had pieces of shirt and trousers, but even these were pinned together with small sharp sticks. They had nothing to eat for a week, and not one cent in money.

Since we have been on the River we have worked from half-past two and three o'clock in the morning till nine and ten at night. Besides this you go home to your shanty at night, tired and wet, and have to cook your beans before you can eat them. And what is this all for? For *gold* of course; but when you wash up at night, you may realize 50 cents, perhaps $1.

It has been raining here steady one week, and the mountains are all covered with snow. Give my respects to old friends and tell them to be contented and stay home.[11]

Charles Major's letter advanced a common theme. On the eve of the Cariboo gold rush, of the 30,000 hopeful miners who had stampeded to the Fraser, some 25,000 left penniless. Those who had money found their way back to the saloons of Lillooet, Yale and Hope for the winter. Here, at least, feuds were better then being frozen.

Native miners who had given up their traditional way of life for the lure of gold fared the worst. Many of them who made their way to the settlements of shanties simply could not afford to eat. Whether it was their neglect of laying in winter food stores due to the craving for the precious metal, or the plunder and damage of traditional food-gathering sites by white miners, is a moot point. Whichever it was, native destitution and starvation was reported from the river from January to April of 1859. What *was* available to them was drink as Douglas's liquor licences had made alcohol cheap. Native women, desperate for money for food, were forced into the white shanties; they became, at best, temporary wives, and at worst, prostitutes to the miners who bided their time until spring snow melt.

In 1860, the Reverend Lundin Brown was sent to Lillooet. He saw degradation, usury and hunger all about him. Brown saw white miners cohabiting with native women, some pregnant. Both women and children, he knew, would soon be abandoned. Brown was beside himself. For the few missionaries like Lundin Brown assigned to the mining camps along the river, the place was one long, strung-out Sodom.

The mainland and island colonies had few white women. Prospectors aside, an 1861 census of the white settlers of the mainland colony revealed 1,456 white males and only 192 white females, some 11% of the total population. In 1855, Governor Douglas estimated the white population of Vancouver Island to be 774. The census for that year revealed that of these, only 265 were white women. In both colonies, many of these women were the settlers' wives; single women could be counted on one's fingers. In Victoria, at the outset of the gold rush, the situation for single men of good breeding was difficult, to say the least. In August 1858, Lieutenant Charles Wilson of the Royal Engineers went to a ball given by the officers of the HMS *Plumper*; he was not encouraged by what he saw:

> We met all the young ladies of Vancouver Island, they only numbered about 30 and are not very great beauties, however, I enjoyed myself very much not having had a dance for such a time. Most of the young ladies are half-breeds and have quite as many of the propensities of the savage as of the civilized being.[12]

In the goldfields of the mainland colony, the situation was even worse. Dr. Friesach, a noted mathematician and gentleman tourist from Austria, travelled to Yale to see the fabled diggings. He found the place and its inhabitants repugnant. Nonetheless from a shack marked "American Restaurant," his calculations caused him to estimate that Yale was bulging with over 3,000 inhabitants. One thing was certain; there weren't enough women:

Americans were undoubtedly in the majority ... then followed Germans, French, and Chinese. Next came Italians, Spaniards, Poles, etc. The feminine population consisted of only six.[13]

D.W. Higgins reported that at a February 1859 dance in Yale:

The few ladies present had no lack of partners, while most of the men were forced to dance with each other. All the ladies wore hoops at that ball, and how in the world they contrived to make their way through the crowded hall and retain their skirts will ever be a mystery to me.[14]

Of course, a fist-fight ensued over the choice of the man who would sit at the one ladies' table.

It was the same everywhere. Dr. Cheadle, medical attendant to the eccentric English epileptic Lord Milton, had visited the goldfields while the Reverend Brown was in Lillooet. Milton and Cheadle found themselves holed up one night in a cheap Port Douglas roadhouse, and Dr. Cheadle noted a situation familiar to Friesach:

A vile hole ... put up overnight at MacDonald's [roadhouse], a wretched supper of pork and liver, miners gambling and drinking ... Yankees pondering the scarcity of women.[15]

George Hills, the Bishop of Columbia, was, as others, galled about the mixed-blood marriages á la façon du pays. While travelling to a roadhouse at Seton Lake with Reverend Brown in 1861, Hills met the innkeeper's dark-skinned wife and tried valiantly to rationalize her native origins:

> I rode over to Mr. Calbraith's [*sic*] at Seton Lake. He is the owner of a steamboat and an American. They had prepared dinner. Mrs. Calbraith is a particularly pleasing and ladylike person. She is descended from the Cherokee Indians ... though with seven parts of white blood.[16]

Sexually available native women readily filled the void created by the dearth of white women and it incensed those who tried to minister to the frontier communities. An appeal to the latent Christian morality of a white miner cut little ice, for these were hard men, who would not easily let their small comforts be taken from them by sanctimonious clerics. More, an aboriginal woman who happened to be a partner of a white miner or settler did not feel bound by the same conventions of monogamy and marriage as espoused by the missionaries. Most white, God-fearing citizens considered such women to be disease-ridden, alcoholic and too readily given to abortion. To the frontier cleric and his bishop, such a "klooch" was an affront to the belief in the pious and obedient Christian wife. It didn't take long to demonize aboriginal women who, with stoic indifference, stood opposed to everything deemed holy by those believing in God and the idea of Empire.

Many men had thoughts as to what could be done, but only a few put their careers on the line to do it. Strangely, the first was neither a missionary nor a Christian. In 1859, Selim Franklin was a member of the Vancouver Island House of Assembly. Well aware of Victoria's burgeoning migrant population, he had campaigned on a platform of road-building, land reform, and female immigration. Certain proceeds of all land sales should, Franklin asserted, "be applied to encourage emigration, with the preference given to respectable females."[17] The press took this energetic bachelor politician and Jew to task for his vision, mocking his marital status and his race in the process. "Preference over whom? And whence Mr. Franklin's special anxiety on this point? Is he tired of single blessedness, but afraid to plunge into matrimony until servant girls' wages are lowered?"[18] Despite the attack, Selim Franklin was elected; two years later he was on the hustings again with the same argument. Ever the media hound, Franklin addressed the House of Assembly in October of 1861, claiming that female immigration would do much to settle Victoria's raucous throng of migrants, which apparently did not appeal to many of the city's new inhabitants. He was not re-elected.

If a far-sighted politician, a few gentlemen travellers and many bachelor miners were distressed by the shortage of white women on the frontier, the effect of the situation was even more worrying to the missionaries. They knew what the abundance of young aboriginal girls meant in the mining camps. For a man of the cloth, white cohabitation with native women was simply a transgression of God's Law and in Lillooet, the Reverend Lundin Brown, who felt this damnation and saw first-hand its ensuing violence, prayed for a solution. Christianity alone, he came to understand, was not enough for these men. Young and unmarried himself, Brown also met many single, good men as he ministered to the miners in the diggings along the river. In shacks, shanties, pubs and tents, wherever he held a meeting, a few prospectors came forward and talked of their loneliness. They told him they lived with native women only because good Christian English women were not available. Suddenly a prayer was answered; where Selim Franklin had failed, the Reverend Lundin Brown thought he might succeed.

Late into the dark nights of the winter of 1861, by light of oil-lamp, the earnest bachelor missionary, with the faith of a new-found idea in his heart, began to pen some very long letters home.

Chapter Three
Prophets and Pilgrims:
Missionaries in the Goldfields

Who would true Valour see,
Let him come hither;
One here will constant be,
Come Wind, come Weather;
There's no discouragement
Shall make him once relent
His first avowed intent ...
To be a Pilgrim.[1]

The Reverend John Sheepshanks was a whistler. He whistled all the time, the grand old hymns as well as popular tunes of the day. John Sheepshanks was no ecclesiastical high brow; in fact, he was just the opposite. This cheerful, gangling, red-haired prelate thought that the whole missionary enterprise was one great adventure. He drove his more proper superior, the Reverend Dr. George Hills, Bishop of Columbia, crazy with all his whistling.

"I cannot think how you can indulge in that habit of whistling," Bishop Hills used to say to him. "It is so undignified. I might say so un-clerical."[2] Yet it was Sheepshanks's lightness, his lack of pomposity, that the solemn Dr. Hills did not understand. Whistling gave this friendly, giant cleric a genuine connection with the miners on the frontier. The six-foot, three-inch eccentric didn't rest on High Church ceremony; he remained throughout his time in the goldfields the quintessential country vicar. Full of *noblesse oblige*, wry humour and youthful goodwill, John Sheepshanks simply overflowed with faith.

The Society for the Propagation of the Gospel had sent the 25-year-old minister from Leeds to the new Crown colony of British Columbia in 1859. In all, seven Anglican missionaries came within a year, all young men in their late 20s. Most knew each other from Oxford, Cambridge or Edinburgh, or became close friends through their common task on the frontier. They all thought they would change the world and for a while there was little church infrastructure to interfere with their heartfelt idealism.

Some years before the arrival of the bride-ships, Anglican missionaries had been sent out to establish a beachhead in the gold-rich colony west of the Rockies. Britain considered their work no less important than the task of the colonial administrators or the Royal Navy. The missionaries themselves were inspired not only by their faith, but also with the knowledge that they were *English*. They were the advance guard of British imperialism, agents of the Empire, upholders of the Faith and makers of History.

If the Victorian era was a time of growing religious doubt for some people, it was, for imperial regimes such as Britain and France, also a time of intense missionary activity. The exploits of the missionaries in Britain's far-flung colonies were followed by the faithful at home with the same passion as groupies have today for their super-star idols.

In England, the adventures of the missionary and explorer Dr. David Livingstone had captured public attention for a full 30 years. He converted the African people around Lake Tanganyika and mapped the mysterious Zambesi and Congo rivers. When Livingstone was believed lost on one of his missions, Henry Morton Stanley set out to find him with the same spirit later invested in the search for the Arctic explorer Sir John Franklin. When Livingstone was found, his adventures made him one of the most popular heroes of the day. His work in Africa gave the activities of other Anglican missionaries a glamour that attracted still more earnest young Englishmen to the missionary life.

And what an attraction that life had become. Inspired, the missionaries had swept across the South Pacific islands as the 19th century began and by 1818, in British North America, they were already well beyond Quebec. By the 1820s, the Anglican Church had established its huge diocese of Rupert's Land at Red River, and by the 1840s, Catholic and Anglican missionaries were fighting it out for territory and souls on Vancouver Island. The native peoples, who had lived as hunter-gatherers for thousands of years in the remote regions of the north and west, would have schools and Christian missions; like a wheatfield full of locusts, the area was crawling with missionaries.

The Reverend John Garrett, the man who read Lundin Brown's letter to the members of the Columbia Mission Society that February evening in 1862, had good reason to be proud. It was the Columbia Mission that had continued the work that the Society for the Propagation of the Gospel had begun. By 1862, Victoria and the goldfields of the Fraser and the Cariboo were bursting with prospectors, and the Anglican Church had kept pace. The missionaries Richard Dowson and James Dundas were both sent to Victoria. Colleagues Charles Woods and Richard Lowe soon followed them and established there the first Anglican boys' school. John Garrett's brother, Alexander, was assigned to work with native children on the Saanich Peninsula, while James Gammage began a mission in Port Douglas at the end of Harrison Lake. David Pringle preached in Hope, and the Reverend Crickmer ministered to men working the gravel bars up the Fraser River. James Reynard headed for Barkerville, while Christopher Knipe and Lundin Brown, who arrived with Bishop Hills, were sent to "Cayoosh" (later Lillooet) and the other mining camps farther upriver. In 1860, the newly installed Bishop of Columbia began to pressure Governor James Douglas for land to be held in church reserves, as well as for money.

Unlike Sheepshanks, who believed in religious adaptability and was delighted to learn about aboriginal culture and cosmology, Bishop George Hills epitomized High Church conservatism. Because he had escaped the yellow fever that swept through his ship, the *Pacific*, on the long voyage out, Hills considered that he had been chosen directly by God for his new task. God hadn't chosen him: Angela Burdett Coutts had. The Christian philanthropist knew Hills while he was rector of Great Yarmouth, one of the richest and most traditional parishes in Britain. She had been impressed with the manner in which he had placed local young lay women in church outreach programs. Miss Burdett Coutts had already funded bishoprics in Australia and Honolulu, and she came to believe that the 43-year-old rector was the right man to promulgate the faith on the colonial frontier. She couldn't have been more wrong.

Bishop Hills arrived in Victoria in 1860, and to his dismay he found that the bustling city was not inhabited entirely by Englishmen as he had expected. He had thought that church government and liturgical law would be the same on the frontier as it had been in hundreds of English parishes for centuries. Hills was in for a shock.

From most accounts, Bishop Hills was a humourless snob. He took an immediate dislike to Governor Douglas, thinking him earthy and uneducated. He wrote of him that he "does not know the tone of a high-minded gentleman ... owing to the fact that he has never lived in England."[3] Hills had some difficulty adapting to frontier conditions, and it marked his tenure as bishop right from the start. His stance toward the relationships between white miners and native women was an important factor in prompting the Reverend Brown's letter to the Columbia Mission Society in London.

In a colony awash with liquor, Bishop Hills espoused temperance. On the strength of rumour alone, he fired a young missionary for allegedly drinking too much on his rough voyage out to the colony. On his forays into the mining camps Hills was totally unsympathetic to the hard-drinking camaraderie that was an essential part of the single miner's life:

> A [certain] man will go into Yale on Sunday & spend twenty-five to forty dollars in drink & treating others. He, himself, though an old miner, never touches spirit, only porter & ale, he always has a dozen of English porter in his house.[4]

On the many gravel bars, Hills approached the miners warily, and he was more than a little unnerved by the presence of their aboriginal women:

> I had conversation with many men as we passed through the extensive [mining] ground. But seldom could I

introduce the subject of religion even indirectly. On passing
a hut we perceived a female inside.[5]

Apart from the sin of cohabitation, Hills firmly believed that
white miners should not be allowed to marry aboriginal women in
a Christian marriage ceremony even if both desired it. For Hills, a
native woman was a heathen who satisfied only the "grosser
appetites" of the miner. The best he could do for the men in the
mining camps who wished to legitimize their mixed-blood
relationships was to advise his missionaries to conduct a civil
marriage ceremony. Hills thought a heathen woman must first be
fully converted, before being granted the privileges of marriage
with a Christian ceremony.

White women on the other hand were, to Hills, above reproach.
He believed them to be the embodiment of goodness and
obedience. He had allowed women to help shepherd the
parishioners at home, but only at the call of male High Church
superiors. Hills was afraid that native women would lead white
men away from the highly stratified English society of order, civility
and faith, of which he was at the pinnacle. The good bishop made
sure, when he arrived on the frontier, that his underlings shared
this understanding. Reverend Lundin Brown accepted Hills's
position completely, while John Sheepshanks thought his austere
outlook took all the fun out of the missionary experience.

Back in that free, high summer of 1859, before the bishop's arrival,
Sheepshanks had already travelled up the Fraser River to his first posting
at the small settlement of New Westminster. He recorded his arrival:

I looked up a long stretch of river, and there I saw a bit of
a clearing in the dense Forest. Mighty trees were lying
about in confusion, as though a giant with one sweep of

his arm had mown them down ... between the trees and stumps there were a few huts, one small collection of wooden stores, some sheds and tents, giving signs of a population of about 250 people.[6]

Sheepshanks moved his large frame into a seven-by-ten-foot log cabin, chinked the open cracks with moss and covered a large square hole in the wall with a piece of old calico. He considered himself "quite well off"[7] when he noticed with a chuckle that his prospecting neighbour had used gin bottles for glass in the crude, cut-out window of his own little shack.

Sheepshanks called his flock to his first service in the local customs house with a borrowed Chinese gong. When only seven came, he promptly wrote his friends in Cambridge who sent enough money for the design and construction of the first real split-log church in the mainland colony. Sheepshanks cajoled Governor Douglas to lay the cornerstone and persuaded the Royal Engineers to design and build it. When Holy Trinity Church was completed, Colonel Moody had his Royal Engineers march to each Sunday service in full dress uniform. The place was packed.

"They were all spit and polish," Sheepshanks noted, "and the singing was good."[8]

The affable young Yorkshireman was most comfortable, however, on the circuit. With his hands in his pockets, his wide-brimmed hat, clerical collar, corduroy trousers and hob-nailed boots, Sheepshanks would sit, feet dangling, astride his old horse and plod through the mining camps whistling away to high heaven. His innocent airs echoed up the length of the river as he worked his way from New Westminster to the interior.

John Sheepshanks and his friends, Christopher Knipe and Lundin Brown, were all highly educated men. Like most Church of England missionaries they were the sons of the upper class and had taken degrees in theology, Greek and literature. They had chosen a life in the church partly because the alternatives — a commission in the army and the blood-red ravines of Sebastopol, or the slow death of teaching school — held no appeal. At least being a country vicar in one of the thousand parishes of England's green and pleasant land held the promise of a decent life. For them, a stint of missionary work in the colonies promised an adventurous start. Unlike many men, Sheepshanks, Knipe and Brown all volunteered for a period of five years. They took no salary.

Of the three, Brown was the least fit for his term on the frontier. Unlike Sheepshanks, he was earnest to a fault. His father had been a minister, so a life in the church was an implicit expectation. He had finished his degree in Classics at Edinburgh in 1854, then ministered in Largo, Florida, for five years. At 29, he volunteered for British Columbia as soon as the call came.

Having created the mainland colony, the British Crown had its work cut out. They had to transform a scrambling, fur-trade and gold-rush society into a more civilized place in which natives, miners and settlers could live together peaceably. With government backing and the support of the general public, England's men of faith would lead the charge. However, the generations-old native encampment at Cayoosh, where Brown began his mission, would be overrun with miners and, within two years, be transformed into the raucous, anti-clerical gold town of Lillooet.

Brown had been provided with two clear objectives. In the best tradition of mid-19th-century evangelism, he must first extricate the natives "from the awful superstitions in which they were now sunk."[9] Secondly, he was directed to "win the attention of men, whose acute minds had discovered the difficulties of belief, and whose callous hearts were deeply alienated from the life of God."[10]

Brown saw the natives as noble savages and initially blamed the fur traders for the corruption that he saw all about him:

> Long ago, perhaps a century back, there came down the [Fraser] river a boatload of pale faces ... They spent two days with the Lillooets and were treated with hospitality. In return for this, they taught those simple savages strange and false things. First that it was religious to dance ... the writer [Brown] has known those Indians to spend a whole night, from dawn to dusk, furiously leaping and dancing. Next, they taught them that it was wrong to have only one wife; two, at least, every good Indian ought to have.[11]

He believed that young native women, whom he tried to convert, were a constant source of temptation. As innocents, Brown believed, they would be readily corrupted by white miners; as libertines, he knew they would be used and discarded by the same men. The trouble was that he kept these feelings inside, until they were vented in his preaching. Most of the miners rejected his carping sermons about mixed-blood relationships, and many felt him to be intrusive and too demanding. Brown, like his bishop, was a serious, devout Christian, too devout, perhaps, for the task that lay ahead. He was also a very bright man, who criticized government apathy when he saw it, and many others in Lillooet respected him for his dedication; all acknowledged the purity of his faith.

John Sheepshanks suffered no such emotional turmoil. In 1860, just before Lundin Brown's arrival, Sheepshanks and his curate friend, Robert Dundas of Victoria, were asked by the Bishop of British Columbia to accompany him on a trip up the Fraser to Lillooet and beyond. George Hills's first responsibility as bishop was to learn about the religious life of the settlements strung along the river like beads on a necklace and his goal was to establish missions and churches in those places he deemed most important. Sheepshanks jumped at the opportunity, and the relish he felt for his task was palpable:

> Traveling in those early days through the interior was primitive, but in fine weather, though laborious, yet very beautiful and very agreeable. Sometimes the forest was very wet. I have occasionally pitched my tent and slept on ground so wet that my feet sank an inch or two into the soft mud. Then one would strew pine leaves on the ground to a depth of several inches ... the scent of the pine leaves was delicious. We never caught cold from the wet surroundings. Indeed, for a healthy man, living in a tent is a preventative of cold.
>
> But a difficulty even greater and more distressing was that of finding fodder for the horses. I was often greatly distressed by the half-starved condition of our poor animal. Multitudes of horses perished on the way to the mines.[12]

At Ashcroft, Sheepshanks and Hills were "entertained by a very delightful Irishman, with all the *bonhomie* and resource of his race."[13] His diary makes no mention of what "resource" the Irishman might have used, though it was probably whiskey.

High on the plateau country beyond Lillooet, Sheepshanks's cheerful resourcefulness and natural compassion made him popular and welcome among the natives. He had already seen the early ravages of smallpox among them on the lower Fraser and he had come to the Cariboo well prepared. He had asked Dr. Seddall of the Royal Engineers to teach him the new art of vaccination:

> Sitting upon a fallen tree and taking out my lancet
> [hypodermic syringe], I told the chiefs that I wished to cut
> them all slightly in the arm and put in a little good medicine
> which … I tried to express myself carefully … would
> preserve them from the bad disease. It was a matter of
> simple faith for the Indians, who had never heard of
> vaccination, but were quite prepared to take my word. So
> they formed themselves into a line — there were about
> eighty of them — in order of dignity.
> First came the head chief; then his wife, then his daughter,
> then the chief second in rank, and so forth …[14]

Preaching to them, after that, was easy, though using the Chinook
jargon to do so was something else:

> It was difficult to speak to these dear people through such
> a poor medium [Chinook] whereby one could do little more
> than state facts, such as those of the Apostle's Creed. Yet
> though the preaching was so imperfect, it was delightful and
> very touching to see with what gladness these wild,
> untaught people received the Word.
> The painted faces that a while ago looked stern, almost
> threatening, are now changed, and soft expressions play now
> upon their features. The eyes that were so wild now look calm
> and gentle; and the old people nod their heads, and with shut
> eyes exclaim, "Klosh, klosh, klosh (It is good; it is good)."[15]

Sheepshanks and Dundas began preaching to the prospectors
where they found them, in the restaurants and saloons of the mining
camps. When the owners of these establishments turfed them out
for fear of losing a morning's profit, they continued religious services

in makeshift cabins and tents. They buried miners who had died from accident, exhaustion, typhoid or tuberculosis, and befriended many who needed consolation. Sheepshanks genuinely admired the sociability among the miners, and noted how many of them thought nothing of walking ten miles to pay their last respects to one of their comrades. In turn, the miners treated him well and often joked kindly about the inexperience of this towering tenderfoot.

The natives soon taught Sheepshanks how to spearfish for salmon. When the Fraser River froze all the way to Hope in the awful winter of 1862, he played a form of ice hockey with storekeepers, gold commissioners, miners and aboriginals alike. His journal records how he plastered his friend Knipe with snowballs, and used a frozen sponge to nail up a window-cloth that had blown in on him in his cabin during one particularly cold night.

Sheepshanks also taught many of the Chinese miners to read English. More, he had brought out his own large collection of books for the miners and established a portable lending library. When he could, he talked of Cambridge and ideas to other highly educated men who found themselves intellectually starved in the vastness of the Pacific slope:

> Last year when going down country Knipe and I stopped at a wayside house, a wretched hovel, where the only food that we could get was American beans and bread. There was no woman in the house as usual.
>
> A young man with a wild head of hair ... [who] was the landlord and did all the work was a Cambridge Senior Optime. Having the curiosity to see in the morning what book it was with which he beguiled his time, I found it was "Goodwin's Course of Mathematics".[16]

Sheepshanks, as other missionaries, would be confronted with the thorny role of women and their erstwhile relationships almost as soon as he arrived:

> On one occasion when I was walking down a Creek to see a sick miner, I met a man and a [white] woman coming up. "Wal Doc, me and this woman were coming up to look for you. We want to know if you can marry us?" "Oh yes, certainly, if all is right, and after proper notice." "Wal, y'understand, it is only for the season."[17]

Sheepshanks didn't marry them, not because it suited only their immediate desires or ruffled his own values, but because they were both drunk. A week later when the same woman wandered off a trail and was lost, he organized a party of miners to search for her. "This was enough to arouse the Creek. No matter under such circumstances about her character, she was a woman; that was enough."[18] When the woman was found four days later in the bush far from the trail, she had gone quite mad.

For Sheepshanks, the woman's madness was a double loss. She had acted outside the Christian vows of matrimony and she had lost her virtue. But it was not her lasciviousness that troubled Sheepshanks; it was the fact that she had operated outside church law. Sheepshanks prayed for the tormented soul of the estranged woman for a very long time. His view of women, like that of his contemporaries, required that they be obedient servants to the demands of Christianity. On this, he and Hills firmly agreed. Christian obedience meant that women should be the compliant agents of the clergy and subordinate to their men. All Anglican missionaries and most white Anglican Victorians believed strongly that God was right to punish Eve for tempting Adam to fool around in the Garden of Eden. Sheepshanks's lost woman, like Eve, was a poor soul who had wandered away from her man.

For most Victorians, the idea of womanhood was placed high on a pedestal. For Victorian Christians, a woman was grace personified. For Victorian evangelical missionaries, the notion of womanhood was bound up in the very embodiment of Christ himself. Lundin Brown wrote, "The son of Mary still reveals himself through women, and through her puts forth His healing and civilizing grace."[19] Such idealization became, for many Victorian women themselves, too much of a limitation and this constraint was certainly one factor in early feminist organizations.

Yet to the faithful, a lost Victorian woman was the epitome of degradation. Brown, Sheepshanks and most other men of the mid-19th century idealized women to an impossible standard. A male, especially on the frontier, could get away with his vices, but it was believed that a servile, domestic, good Christian woman could save him. As dominant as men were in the Victorian period, the frail, virtuous young maiden was still expected to grow up and become the matriarch of the Christian family. She was the one who would bear and raise the children, and nourish them in the faith. This uncompromising position was one of the factors that made the wife experiment of the bride-ships a crashing failure from the outset. Many of the street-wise orphans, working girls and educated gentlewomen who emigrated on the church-sponsored vessels were certainly not going to buy into this familiar expectation in a land of little history and less class.

John Sheepshanks understood and accepted the strained, hard life of men in the goldfields, but neither he nor Lundin Brown could accept the conjugal equality in female aboriginal and white male cohabitation. The best they could do was to accept the equality of their lost souls.

Lundin Brown was not as forgiving. His initial enthusiasm to convert the hardened, independent miners around Lillooet was soon dampened by a sobering dose of real life in the goldfields. The men working the sluice-boxes liked the readily available aboriginal women, cared little about organized religion and appreciated even less the particular brand of revivalism that Brown was pushing. Unlike Sheepshanks in New Westminster, Brown found little interest in Hills's decision to construct a church, even among the town's more conservative businessmen. By mid-summer of 1862 he was feeling utterly depressed. He wrote that "churches and church-going might be well enough in an old settled country, but they were quite unsuited for a new one, where men came to get gold, and were content, for the time, to worship no other god."[20] It took a full year for Brown to persuade the town's magistrate and his committee to erect St. Mary's, the first small church in the district. When the church opened on Christmas Day, Brown realized with growing cynicism that many of the parishioners were more interested in the increased property values generated by its stabilizing influence than in having a place of worship.

Even after five years, interest in St. Mary's never really caught hold, and it troubled Brown deeply. Miners hardly ever attended of their own volition, and the earnest young pastor was required to make regular rounds of the "billiard-saloons" and the "squaw-dance establishments" in all kinds of weather, coaxing individuals to "receive God's Truth."[21] On such occasions, Brown noted:

> The saloon-keeper would say, "Waall, boys, here's the parson come again, to ask you to go to church." The answer often was to the effect, "Waall, I guess some of us will give him a call tonight."[22]

On another occasion Brown bribed a miner to attend church by accepting his challenge to down several pints of lager. Brown won, and the miner and his cronies did attend Sunday services, but only for a short time. In the long run, however, the gutsy little teetotaller found that "nothing could induce [them] to amend their wicked lives."[23] He was aware of their weaknesses and aware too, of the limited effect his exhortations had produced, but he persisted and it made him even more depressed.

Brown found a measure of success in the goldfields outside Lillooet. He visited the sick, attended the dying, prepared those convicted of murder for the scaffold and prayed with those few who came forward, guilt-ridden, over some secret sin. He should have taken solace from these small inroads, as Sheepshanks would have done, but for Brown they weren't enough. His tirades from his pulpit against the miners for their cohabitation with aboriginal women cost him dearly. Once, during Lent in the middle of a particularly fiery sermon, Brown was shouted down by an angry young prospector who protested that even Solomon, with his many wives, was a man after God's own heart.

Feelings ran high, and the following week, not a soul came to church. Later, during his rounds of the saloons, Brown was confronted with cries of "the Church is played out."[24] One saloon owner told him, "You may lead those men, you needn't attempt to frighten or to drive them."[25] The despairing young missionary was shattered.

Each year of his tenure in Lillooet was worse, as other missionaries after Brown soon came to know:

> Lillooet is a terrible place, no rookery in the neighborhood of docks in large cities is so vile. Troops of young girls, whose custom it is to have their fill of vice before marriage,

inhabit the tumble-down cabins; and, men are accustomed to winter at Lillooet on this score alone. Respectable young men, who for years kept away from this habit of society, have at last given in, and are now among the worst.[26]

Brown's evangelism resulted in a dilemma that nearly broke him. If he didn't stand by his religious principles, he could not be a man of the cloth; if he didn't somehow acknowledge white-native sexual relationships, he would lose his small congregations completely.

What saved him from a complete nervous breakdown, and the very real possibility of his being run out of town, was scholarship. In 1862, Brown entered an essay competition that was part of the ten-year anniversary of Queen Victoria's Great Exhibition of 1851. Its organizers in London felt it would be a good idea if visitors to the smaller exhibition could buy an informative pamphlet on Britain's western colonies in North America. There were to be two prizes, one for an essay on Vancouver Island and one for the mainland colony. Brown wrote the mainland essay and won.

His essay was not immediately published, however, due to certain passages that criticized James Douglas's colonial administration. In it Brown wrote:

The backward state of the country, the bad condition of the roads that exist, the waste of the revenue in the construction of roads now abandoned ... and the underdeveloped state of the agricultural resources, are owing to the administration of the Government.[27]

The passage offended Governor Douglas and Brown buckled under the judges' pressure to "clean it up." He changed the passage to read:

The manner in which the Government is carried on and the laws administered, gives general satisfaction. So long as the Colony progresses, and its new necessities are met by new enactments, the colonists (with the exception of an uninfluential clique at New Westminster), are satisfied; they have not the wish, as in the present circumstances they would not have the time to legislate for themselves.[28]

The essay was published by the Royal Engineers Press in New Westminster and was initially well received. However, New Westminster journalists had somehow received the original submission *and* the laundered one, and they published both.

Despite the loss of face and public support, Brown found some peace in his writings and through the pen, he continued to air his feelings toward women, aboriginal and white. His essay on British Columbia proved to be a worthy beginning. More, it also contained the germ of an idea that would lead him out of his double bind. He wrote, "that dissevered from the softening influence of women, men become more or less rough."[29] Brown was referring to his own ideal of the soft, English Victorian maiden who was destined to become the good Christian wife. Brown felt it was only she who could lead her wayward husband out of the wilderness.

In his sanitized, Christianized account of the Chilcotin War, *Klatsassin, A True Story of Colonial and Missionary Life*, Brown further projected his feelings about the root cause of white-native co-habitation. Although he was not impressed by the Chilcotin people overall, he described Klatsassin, the Chilcotin chief, as a noble person with the blue eyes of a European who had acted to prevent acts of native cannibalism. He thought that the Chilcotin women who co-habited with whites had been betrayed through their weakness, and because they lacked the Christian education and worldliness of their European counterparts. In short, Brown came to believe that aboriginal women were either innocent children who were defiled, or youthful temptresses who themselves led the miners astray. Native women, he thought, needed redemption through Christian re-education and the idea of the residential school crossed his mind.

What Brown, Sheepshanks and many other missionaries simply did not understand was the nature of the frontier liaisons between white miners and native women. Brown could not fathom how aboriginal women could be so readily promiscuous and polygamous. In this view, he was not alone. The surveyor David Thompson found the degree of sexual freedom afforded to young women in Indian society scandalous. Thompson was shocked to learn that a native girl still a virgin at 15 was rare. Marriage alliances within aboriginal culture, he soon found, were less about love and individual fulfilment than about reciprocal social and economic arrangements that benefited whole family units. This ancient aboriginal marital custom, ironically less about promiscuity than tribal welfare, was hidden from the missionaries who saw only the sin of free love.

For Brown, as for other missionaries, the moral influence of Christian, English wives and mothers "was the linchpin of religious regeneration."[30] Hence, the moral agenda behind the bride-ships was the idea of mission. Through the bride-ships, lost souls could be brought again to the Christian message.

The Anglican missionaries needed good Christian women to do the work they themselves could not do. The pulpit could not reach into the miners' dark nights, though Brown and others came to believe that a good wife could. At a deeper, more atavistic level, only the good Christian wife could tame the unspeakable sexuality of the reprobate, of which the church was afraid. Paradoxically, as patronizing toward white women as the Anglican Church was, its missionaries needed them to consolidate their own power. So, submissive young English women were to be the real agents of frontier evangelism. Without them, Brown soon came to believe, the Anglican mission was impotent.

Earlier that autumn many miners in the goldfields had left the interior camps along the river for the winter, holing up in Victoria and finding solace from their hard life in the warmth of the available women. The *British Colonist* reported that Victoria's brothels and other "sinks of iniquity"[31] were overrun. As winter wore on into spring and miners began to make their way back up the river, a rumour spread that the Reverend Lundin Brown of Lillooet had ordered boatloads of women for them to marry. Interest in Brown's plan bloomed like snowdrops. The trouble was that the kind of women Brown wanted for his lonely, testy flock was not the kind he received when the bride-ships arrived.

Lundin Brown was disillusioned and in ill health when he left Lillooet in 1865, and for a time no one replaced him. The place grew, "harder, deader, more infidel, more immoral than it ever was."[32] At home, he recuperated for four years, and went finally to minister to the cotton workers of Lichfield in the English midlands, the area that was the source of many of the bride-ships' women. He never married. He spent his final years publishing religious papers and writing about his time in British Columbia, and died in 1876. He was just 45.

John Sheepshanks also left the colony in 1865. He left as he had come, whistling, sauntering, youthful hands in his pockets. He returned to England the long way round, by way of the Pacific Islands where his brother had converted the aboriginal years before. He trekked homeward alone, whistling his way through China, Mongolia, the Gobi Desert, Siberia and on safely through Russia.

At home, Sheepshanks presented public lectures on the "Red Indians of the West." They were popular and full of his astute observations on aboriginal culture and religion. Sheepshanks was not threatened by the native form of pantheism, and he recounted many of their origin legends with the accuracy and admiration of an ethnologist. Ever the affable country parson, Sheepshanks soon took up a post in Bolton, Yorkshire. There, he met and married Margaret Ryott, and with music in his bones, he fathered 13 children.

Chapter Four
FALSE STARTS AND FAINT HOPE

Mrs. Douglas is a good creature, but utterly ignorant: She has no language, but jabbers French or English or Indian, as she is half Indian, half English, and a French Canadian by birth. It would be a great stride for the colony to get a new governor, who might come out with enlightened feelings and ideas, and a lady for his wife.[1]

Edmund Hope Verney, RN, put down his pen and rubbed his eyes. The sharp light from the oil lamp made them water, whenever he worked for too long a stretch. He found his chronometer-watch under a pile of papers on the large navigation table in his cabin. It was already half-past ten, though it could have been later, because it was losing five seconds a day. At the moment, that fact didn't matter because HMS *Grappler* was re-provisioning in Esquimalt Harbour before leaving for Cowichan Bay, and most of the ship's company was on shore leave in Victoria. The first officer understood not to disturb the captain after sundown, so Verney knew he did not have to be careful about leaving his unfinished letter open to the prying eyes of the nosey young lieutenants with whom he met when his ship had its full complement of crew. Verney rose and examined some flowers he had pressed under a heavy volume of nautical tables, took in a long, deep breath from the open porthole, then returned to his seat and continued to work. The letter, dated July 20, 1862, was to his father, and it was marked "private, not to be copied."[2]

Commander Verney had taken charge of HMS *Grappler* just four months before; at 24, this was his first command. Prim, proper and aristocratic to the core, he was the perfect example of the new officer-elite of the Royal Navy. Though trained by those who had served with Lord Nelson's ships-of-the-line at Trafalgar, he understood the technology of steam. *Grappler's* 60-horsepower Maudsley steam engine was as familiar to him as were its three masts and its ability to sail well under canvas alone.

Verney had established himself early as an able career officer. In 1854, he was awarded the Crimean Medal for meritorious service on the gunboat HMS *Terrible* during the Royal Navy offensives at Sebastopol and Odessa. In 1858, he took a naval brigade inland and fought to regain Lucknow for British India. All his commanding officers thought him "zealous and well-conducted,"[3] and his rapid promotion through the ranks was watched carefully by members of the British aristocracy.

Commander Verney loved his appointment to British Columbia, but he was full of criticism for its colonial administrators, their wives and friends. He called Governor Douglas "pompous and ridiculous,"[4] and Attorney-General Carey, "vulgar, unpopular and insincere."[5] Chief Justice Cameron was an "inane booby," and Dr. Helmcken, little more than "an infidel."[6] He remained distant from all the drinking that went on in the officers' quarters and thought privately that it set a bad example. Verney also quietly believed it a calamity that England sent to the island colony many of its prodigal sons who were often wild and went "to the dogs at once."[7] He found solace in the natural magnificence of the coast, and took to collecting various specimens of flora.

If at first glance Commander Verney was an insufferable snob, he came by it honestly. His mother, Eliza, who died in 1857, was a "mighty Protestant"[8] and member of an illustrious naval family. Her father was an admiral who had known Lord Nelson, while her brother, "Uncle Hope," was Sir James Hope, a rear-admiral in the new steam-powered, technology-driven navy. Since he was well connected, it wasn't surprising to find Verney in charge of a gunboat on Her Majesty's far-flung frontier when he was so young.

There was more. Edmund's father, Sir Harold Verney, was a baronet with ancestry dating back to the Cavalier army that supported Charles I. The heir to the huge family estate in Buckinghamshire, Sir Harold was a close friend of the Prime Minister, Lord Palmerston, and as a Liberal parliamentarian he worked beside him to abolish the slave trade. A staunch evangelist and member of the Church Mission Society, Sir Harold supported the charitable work of his second wife, Francis Parthenope, and the nursing work of her famous sister, Florence Nightingale. Sir Harold also knew Angela Burdett Coutts and some said he was behind the appointment of his cousin, George Hills, to the recently created bishopric of British Columbia. Sir Harold had, in fact, attended the February 27, 1862, meeting of the Columbia Mission Society, heard the motion and voted in favour of the creation of its women's emigration scheme. Little wonder then, that the Verneys' eldest son, Edmund, became dutiful, pious and somewhat snooty. More surprising was the manner in which he would find a sense of *noblesse oblige* among those in British Columbia whom he had first disdained. The bride-ships enterprise, which was unfolding thousands of miles away in London, would soon thrust Commander Verney into further prominence.

Verney's comments about the limitations of the native ancestry of the governor's wife reflected the values of his time and the bias of his class. At the core of his scorn was not just the sexual or marital irregularities between white traders or miners and native women; it was due to their lack of a class-consciousness, an absence of deference toward the upper class that was often expressed through these impermanent relationships. Verney abhorred the terrible familiarity that was propagated by frontier mixed-blood relationships, feeling that an Indian presence simply degraded white society, and undercut everything he stood for. He was taken aback by the practice of being addressed by his last name, without his title, and was furious when his uniform was scoffed at by a drunken miner and his "klootch" in the street. Frontier marriages, Verney thought, ignored the social hierarchy upon which an empire had been built.

In these views Verney was not alone. Several of his upper-class officer colleagues had previously voiced what was fast becoming the accepted view. His commanding officer, Vice-Admiral Fairfax Moresby, wrote as early as 1851 that he wanted to see more married men in the colony to curtail the fraternization between white traders and native women. Captain James Prevost of HMS *Satellite* had, in 1854, urged the Church Mission Society to send a missionary to help the Tsimshian natives on the north coast ward off white-aboriginal relationships and "acquire the knowledge and arts of civilized life."[9] The society sent William Duncan. The thoroughly Anglican Lieutenant Richard Mayne, of HMS *Plumper*, had published his experiences in the coastal service in *Four Years in British Columbia and Vancouver Island* in 1862. In it, he wrote that only more white, single women in the colony could prevent inter-racial cohabitation:

> The missionaries find their greatest difficulties when working for the reformation of these people, more particularly as the white trader generally confirms by his practice all that the red man is warned against. If nothing else pleads for the introduction of Englishwomen into British Columbia, this fact surely does.[10]

As these devout and educated officers of the naval establishment began to dine with members of Victoria's landed gentry, a common understanding soon emerged: more single English women in the colony would counter the odious fraternity of bachelor miners who cared little for British traditions, morality or class. On the mainland, this opinion was also gaining support. In 1860, Colonel Moody solicited the British government from New Westminster to subsidize the outward passage of several wives and fiancées of his Royal Engineers so that they might settle in the colony after their initial military duties were over. Moody, and others, understood from first-hand experience that what the miners wanted was not order and British civility, but an excess of whoring, gambling, drinking and gold. The pre-emption of land available only to married couples would, Moody hoped, help counter such activities. In short, the quiet settlement of the colonies was undermined by the hordes of single roughnecks and it became apparent to colonial administrators that what the interlopers needed were good English maidens to tame their anarchic tendencies. Hence, the secular establishment wanted white, single women in the same way as the Anglican Church wanted them — to advance the lifestyle of English conservatism in British

Columbia that had served the gentlemen-class in the old country well, for generations.

At about the same time as Verney and other officer-gentlemen were voicing their views, people in Victoria and the mainland also began to consider the merits of a similar solution. The reason the merchants in the colonies wanted single English women was rooted firmly in their desire for a growing and stable economy. Yet they buried this motive in the more socially acceptable notion of protecting simple family values. On November 30, 1861, the *British Colonist* wrote:

> New countries are far more favorable to matrimony than old ones. Their rapid growth usually affords better opportunities to provide for the wants of a family than old and thickly settled communities.[11]

As evidence, the *British Colonist* proclaimed that since 1859, an unusually high number of 25 marriages had occurred within a two-block area of Victoria. There were, however, problems:

> No sooner does an unmarried woman arrive here than a host of admirers offer to make her happy for life. Still, as we have at least a thousand young men willing to get married, the scarcity of unmarried females is an inducement for parents having large families to make this town their home. One thing is certain — that society here and throughout these Colonies will prove *shiftless* for a long time, except Government or somebody else provides wives for our young men.[12]

Victoria, the *British Colonist* proclaimed, was ready with fine schools, law and order, a highly moral and intelligent workforce and a healthy climate. "We are never visited by epidemics,"[13] they quoted with hubris. The one commodity missing from this optimistic entrepreneurial equation was white, English and female. Lundin Brown's letter, it seemed, had contained an idea whose time had come.

Commander Verney did not harbour his distaste for the local aristocracy for long. Despite his harsh views, he was naturally affable and soon cultivated lasting friendships with the many settlers whom he met on naval patrols. In Victoria, he was full of praise for his relative, Bishop Hills, and became a good friend of the newly arrived Anglican missionary, Reverend Dundas, who also knew Lundin Brown. By early fall, Verney was a regular guest of the Mckenzies, the proprietors of Craigflower Farm. There, he would have dined with the Langfords, the Skinners and local executive officers of the Hudson's Bay Company, and his early uncharitable opinion of Victoria's ruling elite might have been tempered.

Table-talk would have inevitably drifted to the topic of Verney's famous father, who, by mid-summer, was speaking out in the House of Commons about England's emigration policy, and writing of British Columbia in the *Times* of London. These reports attracted much local attention, especially when it came to be known that Sir Harold's son was stationed in Victoria. Of those visiting the Craigflower farmhouse, many came to believe that Sir Harold had become a member of the British parliament's powerful Emigration Committee. Though it was not the case, young Verney, nonetheless, found himself the interpreter of his father's opinions and he wrote many letters home seeking pater's explanation or clarification of his oft-quoted public views. Weekly discussions at Craigflower Manor became lively affairs, and Verney soon became the centre of attention. In his role of go-between, Verney had gained both a voice and a powerful audience. It wasn't long before many of Victoria's elite thought a local organization should be set up to provide for the expected influx of single female immigrants. By mid-August 1862, Edmund Verney was appointed a charter member of Victoria's first Female Immigration Committee.

In the meantime, two actions were under way in England that also prompted the committee to begin its duties. The first was a campaign of articles in *The English Women's Journal* in which two remarkable London feminists sought to redefine the worth of women in Victorian culture and the second was the surprising departure of the first bride-ship, the brigantine *Marcella*.

Beginning in 1858, as statistics of the surfeit of women in English society appeared in the press, Bessie Parkes and Barbara Leigh-Smith set out to challenge the accepted role of women within the institution of marriage. From the outset of their association, Barbara Leigh-Smith believed that a wife's financial dependence upon her husband lowered a woman's dignity and tended to make marriage little more than legalized prostitution. Parkes and Leigh-Smith, who were both wealthy and upper class, wanted women to seek greater responsibility outside marriage, to develop their bodies, to be strong and confident in their own right and gain, at least, some measure of financial independence. The educated, single gentlewoman who sat at home in pater's house and pined for a husband, or was offered a loveless marriage, was an affront to these two activist feminists. They believed that liberation required employment:

Women want work for the health of their minds and bodies. They are placed at a great disadvantage in the market of work because they are not skilled labourers, and are therefore badly paid. They rarely have any training. It is the duty of fathers and mothers to give their daughters this training.[14]

For six years, Bessie Parkes and Barbara Leigh-Smith hammered away in their periodical, challenging under-employed, unfulfilled women to become more involved in educational, social and political reform. They wished the idea of family to change from one of a dutiful wife's sacrifice to an "aggregate of independent interests."[15] Fulfilment, they believed, lay not in marriage and children, but in a more visible, socially active individuality. By 1860, when local emigration agencies throughout Britain were considering sending single women to the colonies, the work of Parkes and Leigh-Smith had done much to persuade a whole class of women, vastly different from the orphan girls gathered by church emigration societies, to strike out alone. Suddenly, despite a public outcry against the feminists, emigration organizers such as Maria Rye could find a willing supply of able women who wanted to opt for a new life. Interestingly, Bessie Parkes soon withdrew from her belief in a fiercely independent, egalitarian activism for women and entered the cloistered, controlling world of the devout Catholic. Here she would find a quieter, "well-ordered charity"[16] that her partner never embraced.

In its heyday, *The English Women's Journal* was popular on both sides of the Atlantic and was read, like the London *Times*, in England and in Victoria. When the educated wives of the colonial administrators in Victoria understood that upper-class English governesses might well be included in any sponsored group of emigrant women, thoughts turned to making worthy preparations.

By the time of Verney's appearances at the Craigflower dinner parties, widespread rumours that certain, well-educated, single women were en route to Victoria took on an aura of truth. The *British Colonist* had already carried news of the Columbia Mission Society's bold scheme, and the *Times* covered the full debate arising from their action plan. In Victoria, the gentry gossiped about the latest developments in the women's independence movement and the goldfields were abuzz with the plans of Reverend Brown. When news reached Victoria that England's Emigration Committee had sponsored passage of a boatload of women bound for Vancouver Island, desire had suddenly become fact. Hopes were dashed when the expected number of English beauties failed to disembark from the *Marcella*, but the reality of the bride-ships enterprise could not, now, be extinguished.

To call the *Marcella* a bride-ship in her own right would be an exaggeration. The trouble was that she was perceived to be one, right from the moment she left London. The reality was that Britain's Emigration Committee had responded only to Colonel Moody's 1860 plea for help in transporting a few wives and fiancées of his Royal Engineers. Most bachelors in Victoria, however, thought that the vessel was loaded to the gunwales with single, available women, and that was enough. The anticipation of their arrival grew with the ever-increasing numbers of fair damsels believed to be on board. The *British Colonist* followed the *Marcella's* slow voyage inward bound:

> Unfounded — The arrival of the ship *Georgiana* yesterday gave rise to a report that the brigantine *Marcella* from London had arrived. There was, consequently, quite a flutter visible for a time among the young bucks, who spruced themselves up with a view of "doing the agreeable" towards the "forty young ladies" said to be aboard.[17]

Doing the agreeable, for the young bucks, meant first staking out a place along Victoria's waterfront, where it was felt the *Marcella* would land. However, the *Georgiana*, inbound from San Francisco, ran in at Esquimalt, and there was the distinct possibility that the *Marcella* might also head there. Tension grew, so a hearty few hiked to an overview of the Esquimalt Basin on May 23 in hopes of more information. It was as if a glimpse of the *Georgiana* might cause the fabled *Marcella* to miraculously appear out of the fog. Hopes fell when the weathered old barque remained alone, well out on a distant anchorage. Loaded even above the bulwarks with 3,000 feet of redwood bound for Nanaimo, the pedestrian *Georgiana* offered nothing. Crestfallen but still optimistic, the dandies returned to Victoria and scanned instead the shipping news of the local papers for information; they correctly deduced that a smaller vessel such as a brigantine would probably be towed right up to the Hudson's Bay Wharf in Victoria's inner harbour. Two days later, with shoes still shined and hearts undimmed, the young bucks learned further disheartening information:

British Vessels Arrived — The brig Marcella, from London arrived at Honolulu April 18, and sailed for this port on the 27th of the same month.[18]

The *Marcella* had been inbound to Victoria for a month, her arrival was imminent and yet she did not appear. The tension could hardly have been more absolute. Suddenly, the miracle:

Arrival of the "Marcella" — The British brigantine Marcella arrived yesterday from London, via the Sandwich Islands, she was 160 days in reaching Honolulu, and 32 days from the latter port to Victoria.[19]

The *Marcella* was a small, slow, two-masted, 200-ton coastal trader built in Prince Edward Island in 1856, and this epic voyage had taken six and a half months. Bought originally by Holman and Sons of Exeter, to carry goods from the markets of the West Country and Cornwall to London, the *Marcella* was stoutly built for the inshore vagaries of the English Channel. To take her round the world via Cape Horn, against the prevailing westerlies, then strike out for Hawaii thousands of miles away, was another matter. Captain Porter was lucky to miss the infamous storms near the dreaded Cape Horn, something later bride-ships would meet in full fury. However, his extended long leg to Hawaii across equatorial oceans, in a vessel originally constructed to carry goods and not people in northern climes, would have been a life in hell for the passengers.

That aside, the Hudson's Bay Wharf was filled to overflowing with a crowd of young men eager to catch a glimpse of the "pretty faces and symmetrical figures of the forty blooming English lassies some time since reported to be aboard."[20] Some could not contain their enthusiasm until the tattered brig was alongside and they procured several small longboats beached along the waterway, rowed out and boarded the *Marcella* in mid-channel. The *British Colonist* continued the story:

> When it was found, however, that instead of forty, there were only *four* ladies aboard, a general desire to return to the shore was manifested, and as the vessel reached the wharf, and it was found that a "sell" had been perpetrated, the assemblage disappeared from public gaze as rapidly as snow beneath the rays of a summer's sun.[21]

The truth, when it was revealed, was even harder to bear. Colonel Moody had originally asked Britain's Emigration Committee for financial help for only seven women and six children, the wives and daughters of a few non-commissioned officers who had not been able to afford to emigrate with their husbands. Of those seven, six initially accepted the offer of assisted passage. However, one became seriously ill, while another was "insulted by the suggestion that she would be considered an 'emigrant' or object of charity."[22] When the earnest young dandies found that there were only four women and four children on board, their frustration and condemnation spread rapidly:

> The hoax was a cruel one; and the wretch who could thus wantonly trifle with the affections and feelings of our young bachelors deserves to pass a month in the chain-gang. The vessel will commence discharging today.[23]

The real culprit of the *Marcella's* disappointing cargo was not any single person. Rather, it was a function of miscommunication that wasn't surprising given the state of world-wide communications in 1861. Flag semaphore between merchant vessels at sea was unreliable at best and steam-assisted mail ships were slow. Other than snippets of news carried from port to port by wandering traders, a ship at sea was alone with her story for the duration of her voyage. International telegraphy was in its infancy. Besides, meaningful interaction between the mainland and island colonies in British Columbia throughout this period was well nigh impossible. "Columbia hates Vancouver Island,"[24] Verney wrote in 1862 and information destined for New Westminster about inbound single women would hardly be passed on. The differences in economics, class, racial make-up, population and rivalry kept the two colonies feuding with each other until long after their union in 1866, and British Columbia's confederation with Canada in 1871.

A full year had passed since the fiasco of the *Marcella*, and no other shipload of single ladies graced Victoria's shores, but on August 6, 1862, Victoria's Female Immigration Committee felt it should meet for the first time. Commander Verney was pleased with the committee and felt confident that it could thwart further disorder. He dutifully passed on to his father the preliminary proposals the committee had made, and didn't hesitate to impart his personal doubts about the whole bride-ship venture.

Initially Verney felt that "not more than a half-a-dozen women will go to Columbia; [as] the gold-possessors will come to Victoria."[25] Verney believed, too, that only a few miners would remain and marry, leaving many girls stranded. In this light, the committee proposed that the few Victoria families who had applied for a servant-girl should pay a large registration fee, along with the addition of a monthly subscription rate to care for a young woman should she be abandoned. The upper-class representatives of Victoria's Female Immigration Committee were certainly not going to entertain any philanthropic notions of taking in England's poor.

The Victoria committee instructed Verney to find out "on what basis or authority your [English] committee is founded? Is it purely Church of England? Does it send emigrants to the colony or to the mission?"[26] Verney was to add that, "We have agreed to receive them for the colony, not for the mission."[27] Though some on the committee believed that a payment from England would accompany the women's arrival, Verney wrote, "We are inclined to accept these women as a free gift from the people of England, and to believe that they do not expect to be repaid."[28] He ended his letter with a personal note:

> I myself have personal doubts as to the great want of
> women in these colonies, and have an idea that all the money

we can get here, will be absorbed in maintaining for a time those women for whom situations cannot at once be found: in any case it would be madness to send out more women until it has been seen how this experiment answers. [29]

Verney knew that another boatload of sponsored English lasses had left England on the *Tynemouth* on the 10th of June, but believed that the estimated time of arrival, assumed to be during the last two weeks of September, was wholly inaccurate. Speaking as a naval officer of considerable experience, Verney stated that it was completely impossible that the *Tynemouth* could arrive before the middle of October. The committee accepted his expertise and adjourned, content to wait for more information on the vessel and its prized cargo. Just below the horizon steamed a cruel surprise.

Despite the public frustration felt over the *Marcella* incident, many bachelors in Victoria had not completely given up their enthusiasm that other bride-ships would soon arrive. Many eyes continued to roam both the horizon and the small print of the local papers. Such vigilance paid off on the morning of September 11, 1862, when the *British Colonist* offered yet another glimmer of hope:

> The *Seaman's Bride*, from Australia, with about twenty females destined for this place, put in at that port [San Francisco], for provisions and water. [30]

Deflation followed as they read on. The females never made it to British Columbia. When the run-down barkentine arrived in San Francisco on September 2, all the unescorted young women on board jumped ship and disappeared into the night. Victoria's press, woefully ignorant of the details, continued the story:

And what did the Yankees do? Alas! They captured the affections of the girls and induced them to remain there, while the vessel came on to this port without even a petticoat to delight the eyes and cheer the palpitating hearts of the Victorians, who were preparing to receive the young ladies with open arms.[31]

The girls were, in reality, convicted prostitutes who were deported from Australia "to rid the ... colonies of their unwanted presence."[32] Their untimely disembarkation in San Francisco was only the beginning of a much larger story that shocked Victoria as much as the loss of the so-called beguiling petticoats.

The "Seaman's Bride" Case

In the Police Court, yesterday, the captain of the Seaman's Bride appeared, obedient to the summons issued upon the complaint of ill-treatment preferred against him by his Australian passengers. Attorney-General Carey, instructed by Mr. Bishop, appeared for the prosecution, and Mr. Courtney for the defense.[33]

An unheard-of number of passengers, 65 in total, had filed suit against Captain Wyman for breaches in the maritime Passenger Act. The charges included a lack of proper meals for passengers on the five-month voyage due to insufficient quantities of potatoes, suet and oatmeal. The bully beef, taken on board in Melbourne, was already rank with rot and the flour was said to be crawling with maggots. It was alleged that passengers were continually served rancid butter, while the required daily dose of lime juice, given to all to ward off the still troublesome scurvy, never materialized. Beyond this, the plaintiffs asserted that the fresh-water supply ran out eight days before the vessel reached port. Wyman was also charged with ignoring the international laws of quarantine that stipulated passengers must be held on board for 48 hours after arrival, before being allowed to disembark.

Breaches in the Passenger Act were not uncommon. However, by the 1860s with increasing emigration to Britain's colonies around the world, allegations against sea captains who brazenly refused to feed passengers properly or to provide medical attention were being treated as a serious contravention of maritime law. Basic nutrition, especially on a three-to-six-month ocean crossing, was critical in preventing ship-borne disease. Britain might have been hemorrhaging with the loss of its citizens but its liberal-minded parliamentarians were not going to let them die en route to its colonies and it was expected that the colonies would enforce the Passenger Act.

However, the voice of the far right in Victoria was, at the outset, more concerned with bemoaning the loss of revenue that the news of such a lawsuit might create than feeling concern for the poor souls who had suffered at sea. The *British Colonist* reported:

> We feel a deep interest in opening trade with Australia. If ships bring from there a nominal freight in passengers with the design of taking in a return cargo of lumber, let the captain and ship be given to understand that the Passenger Act cannot be violated with impunity. But to reach that end, three or four suits are all that are really necessary.
>
> We cannot consent that passengers who have been maltreated on a voyage shall go without redress; but at the same time it is desirable to protect the shipping interests against the principle of having numberless suits brought

against ships merely to subserve the interests of members of the legal fraternity.[34]

Captain Wyman was outraged at the charges and wrote to the papers charging vilification and ignorance.

To a Royal Navy officer like Commander Verney, the trial was a sobering initiation into a world of which he had little direct experience. Captain Wyman, Verney knew, would surely have faced court marshal and possible imprisonment were he in the purview of the Admiralty. As a member of the committee overseeing the arrival of the bride-ships, Verney was most aware of his responsibility toward the women involved. As the ex-officio magistrate on the case, the last thing on his mind was the loss of income that a few maritime entrepreneurs might suffer should a harsh judgment be brought.

The case of the *Seaman's Bride* prompted Verney to investigate conditions on the emigrant ships. What he found unnerved him completely.

Beginning in the mid-1840s, old, full-rigged ships, long overdue for a refit, sailed regularly for Australia, New York, California or Quebec. Consigned to the damp and darkened decks below, destitute emigrants in steerage had little in the way of accommodation. Those who were lucky would find row upon row of makeshift, open, wooden-planked double bunks. These would be torn apart and stored deep in the bowels of a ship at the end of each trip, as the holds were filled with ore, lumber or wool for its return voyage. Such temporary structures were ill conceived, slapped together, uncomfortable and often dangerous. When a vessel was overcrowded it was common practice that two unmarried women would be forced to share a single bunk. Life below decks was little more than one large communal dormitory.

Maritime law in the early 19th century demanded only that steerage passengers be provided with drinking water and a place (not a berth) to sleep. Cooking was a collective activity, done in large pots on a contained but open fire-pit, and ventilation, especially in inclement weather, was impossible. Privacy was non-existent, sanitation was only rudimentary and women would have felt it more than most. Toilet cubicles made of old sail-canvas were outfitted with only a sea-bucket and had to be carried regularly through the sleeping quarters, up to the deck and emptied over the side.

In the days before the Passenger Act of 1847, food for the long ocean passage was brought on board by passengers themselves. Potatoes, onions, hard-tack biscuits, oatmeal, perhaps some pickled eggs and a shared old shank of beef, were bought or bartered for on the waterfronts of Liverpool or Queenstown. Most meals aboard were stews, boiled daily in common cooking pots, accompanied by a piece of hard-tack bread. Smoke from the open fires made the air below heavy, yet it did hide the other smells.

When the ship-owners were finally ordered to provide rations, more often than not it was salt beef or mutton, simply doled out to steerage passengers who had to cook it for themselves. There would be no fruit. Straw could be had for the makeshift berths but it, too, must be purchased on board. When mattresses and bolsters were available, they were old, well used and smelled of decay. Old coats became blankets and in a short time, all clothing became fetid. When in foul weather the poor, seasick souls couldn't make it to the bucket or to the deck, mattresses and straw rotted and became full of urine and vomit. Epidemics lurked in the moaning darkness.

The financially strapped owners and underpaid captains of these once-proud tall ships treated the humanity crammed below with less dignity than the cattle or the slaves that these same old ships had carried in an earlier era.

A three-month sailing voyage in the mid-19th century around Cape Horn to Victoria or San Francisco was a time rife with misery and disease. One steerage passenger noted that all the corners of the decks deep below were "filled with every sort of filth, broken biscuits, bones, rags, and refuse of every description, putrefying and filled with maggots."[35] The stench, spoilage, condensation, dead air, cold and lack of nutrition all took their toll. If the diet of boiled, salted meat and potatoes was hard for the adults to swallow, it was a killer for the children. With provisions fatally deficient in vitamins and without fresh milk, children weakened by shipboard diarrhea would waste away and die. In 1853, on a passage out to Australia, Henry Knight watched 50 infants die from starvation and dehydration before his own children, first a son and then a daughter, succumbed.[36] Typhus, tuberculosis, smallpox or pneumonia would wipe out whole families. Often whole ships were decimated. The situation was so bad that by the 1840s, America fined its skippers ten dollars for every corpse brought ashore. Burials at sea became both expedient and common, and it was said that ten percent of all steerage passengers died en route. Some relatives were able to scavenge a piece of old sail-cloth for the shroud of their beloved; others were not so lucky. These slow, floating slums, full of people at the edge of desperation, were ticking time bombs of anarchy.

As witness after witness told their sad story to the court, on behalf of the 280 passengers on board the *Seaman's Bride*, Verney and police magistrate Augustus F. Pemberton were numb with disbelief. Verney found himself thinking of the fate of the young women on the *Tynemouth*; they were as much *his* responsibility as anyone's, and the vessel was slowly heading his way.

Verney was pleased with his appointment on the case, and accepted that the trial required a background in maritime affairs that a simple police magistrate would not have. However, there were citizens in Victoria who felt they did not need yet another colonial overlord in the guise of a "naval" magistrate to interfere with its administration of civil justice:

> Editor British Colonist — Can you inform us by what authority the Commander of H.M. gunboat "Grappler" takes a seat on the "Bench" of Magistrates?[37]

Questions flew. Where would the colony be, should the *Grappler* be suddenly called away? What was the commander's primary loyalty, the Admiralty, or the democratic civil authority on Vancouver Island? Verney's ex-officio appointment raised a storm of protest. Notions of political sovereignty, and the phrase "who shall have dominion" began to have sway:

> We think His Excellency [Gov. James Douglas] could find competent men who reside in Victoria to perform the duties of magistrates without appointing a naval officer on full pay ... You are really a strange set of people on this island. Your colony is un-English, and your acts, both official and judicial, are a disgrace to a British Colony ...[38]

Commander Verney may have been an aristocratic stuffed shirt, but he knew his duty. Captain Wyman was found guilty and fined a total of £145 and with costs, he would have lost about £300 which, in 1862, would have represented almost twice his annual salary. The judgment also raised the spectre of impropriety in Wyman's association with the men and women in steerage, as

Verney fined him dearly for "selling spiritous liquors to steerage passengers."[39] Wyman accepted his conviction with grace, and though he thought Verney was wrong in his judgment, he didn't blame him for his view. In fact, Wyman was reported as being complimentary toward the naval commander behind his back and, as Verney wrote, "was sure I had acted conscientiously."[40] On September 20, 1862, the *Seaman's Bride* left Victoria, never to return.

However, just three nights before, completely unannounced and a month early, the *Tynemouth* had quietly dropped anchor in Esquimalt Basin. The stories its passengers would tell made the strange case of the *Seaman's Bride* seem like a Sunday-school picnic and Verney was in it, up to his neck. The work he undertook, on behalf of the young hopefuls who had left England for a better life, made him a witness of this first bride-ships experiment.

Chapter Five
THE VOYAGE FROM HELL: THE *TYNEMOUTH*

For all that Mean to Emigrate
Warning take by me
And never go By government
across the raging sea
if a Doctor or a matron
gets you under thair Commands
remember thay Will make you rue
before you reach the land.[1]

Mary McLean, fortunately, was not on the *Tynemouth*, but her short verse, above, speaks volumes about the treatment that she and other passengers suffered under those who managed the emigration of single women to the British colonies in the mid-19th century.

Louisa and Charlotte Townsend sat in the middle of the crowded tender. They were being ferried out to the steam-assisted sailing ship *Tynemouth,* waiting for them on the anchorage in Dartmouth,

Devon. Louisa was 27, Charlotte 25, and they were surrounded by many other single women, most of whom were much younger. No one talked and most huddled low in the small, open boat to avoid the wind. Rain was threatening. Louisa and Charlotte clasped each other's hands tightly and Louisa nervously bit the skin around the thumbnail of her other hand. Only Charlotte stared straight ahead through the drizzle at the black hull of the ship that was to take them half way around the world. They were excited, but they were also afraid.

It had taken them a long time to persuade "Papa" to let them leave for British Columbia, and now it was really happening. Down deep their father, Thomas, understood the need for his girls to strike out on their own. The family had moved to London in his father's time and had prospered. Thomas had inherited family money and his business sense enabled him to provide a large house, servants and a life of privilege for his wife Harriet and his three girls. His two youngest daughters were tutored in sewing, music and French, but they were still unmarried and had no suitors, and employment for Louisa and Charlotte as governesses, in these times of massive unemployment, was out of the question. They were educated gentlewomen soon to be without sufficient means to carry on in their lifestyle and Thomas knew that he had to let his daughters go.

Once he had accepted the inevitable, he arranged for them to travel to British Columbia with the London Female Middle-Class Emigration Society. He was pleased by its association with the Columbia Emigration Society, the new agency created by the Columbia Mission, and was comforted in the thought that his "girls" would be chaperoned. His wife had arranged for Louisa to stay with the daughter of a friend who had emigrated to Victoria years before, so she would begin her new life as a lady's companion. Charlotte, the more outgoing of the two, resisted any such placement and was positive she would soon find work as a governess teaching French and music to the colonial well-to-do. Thomas had given his favourite, Charlotte, the family piano. It was a cabinet model that he had bought in 1837, when Charlotte was five. She had a natural talent and was the best player in the family. Louisa was given the Wheeler and Wilson treadle sewing machine. With their trunks, crammed with clothes, keepsakes and gifts, already loaded on the *Tynemouth* at the London Docks, all that remained were the long last looks toward the small band of people standing motionless, umbrellas in hand, at the wharf.

"Don't worry, Louisa, we'll be fine." Charlotte had noticed her older sister was crying. She put her arm around her. When the tender caught a wave, spray blew over them both.

"I will miss sister so."

"So will I."

They had said good-bye to their older sister at the quayside. She had travelled down to Dartmouth with her husband after the send-off party their friends had given them in London. When Charlotte turned to look back, she had gone.

In the 1860s an ocean voyage to Van Dieman's Land, New York, Quebec or British Columbia might as well have been a voyage to Mars. More often than not, it was a voyage of no return. Families would depart knowing they might never see their loved ones or the land of their birth again. Wills had been drawn up, wine was drunk, tears were shed and, between the endless long hugs, promises made of the regular letters that would be sent home. Beyond this ache remained the immediate anguish of the open sea and the unsettling expanse of the wide, indifferent sky.

It all began when Papa showed Louisa the advertisement for the *Tynemouth* in May. It ran in the *Times* for almost two weeks:

Steam to the GOLD FIELDS of BRITISH COLUMBIA
— Notice to passengers and shippers — For VICTORIA,
Vancouver's Island, (calling if required at San Francisco), the
new iron screw steamship *TYNEMOUTH*, A 1, nine years
at Lloyds, 1500 tons register, and 600-horse power
indicated, ALFRED HELLYER, Commander: will load at
the jetty, London Docks, leaving punctually on the 24th of
May, and embarking passengers at Dartmouth on the 28th of
May. This steamship having just been fitted with new
engines and boilers, as well as all the most recent appliances
made her one of the finest passenger steamers afloat, offers a
mode of transit to the above colony unequalled in speed and
comfort as well as in economy. In order to ensure a rapid
passage she will take only a very limited cargo, touching at
the Falkland Islands for coal, fresh provisions, and water.
The accommodation for the several classes is of a superior
description, the dietary scale liberal, and every means will be
adapted to promote the comfort of the passengers. For
freight or passage apply to W. S. Lindsay and Co., 8
Austinfriars, or 54½ Old Broad St, London.[2]

Essentially, the *Tynemouth* was a three-masted barque outfitted
with a steam engine and a screw propeller. She was heavy, clench-
built over iron frames, 250 feet long. Built in Newcastle-on-Tyne
in 1853, she was commandeered as a troopship in the Crimea, and
gained notice there as the vessel that had survived the savage winter
storm of 1854 on the Black Sea when other like ships foundered.
After her refit in 1860, she boasted three full decks, with second-
and third-class passenger cabins, as in so many similar designs,
behind the tall, slim funnel. On the emigrant ships, second class
was as good as it got.

When the tickets arrived from W. S. Lindsay containing illustrations of company vessels, Charlotte could not believe that any steamship could be so large. Now, on the empty, windy anchorage, she thought the *Tynemouth* looked quite small. She said nothing to her sister.

As the tender drew alongside Charlotte noticed that the *Tynemouth* had retained her original proud figurehead under the long bowsprit, testament to her roots in sail. After nine years of yeoman service, first carrying soldiers, then thousands of emigrants fleeing from England's shores, the *Tynemouth* was beginning to show her age, and the fresh black paint did little to hide the many dents in the upper part of the hull. Above her, she saw that one of the davits that carried lifeboats was bent, and the line rove through the forward block-and-tackle used to haul the tender aboard was frayed almost through.

Once on deck, Charlotte's heart fell as she watched many young men and their families being led below decks. Poorly clad young women, some from the tender, had blankets wrapped around their shoulders and were standing together in small groups near the rail. Soot from the smoking funnel was everywhere, the small hatch-covers that let in light below decks were covered with a thick coat of carbon, and brown, crusty rust had begun to form around many cabin portholes. Though she didn't have the phrase for it, Charlotte understood very quickly that the *Tynemouth* wasn't new at all; she had become, in less than a decade, one of a thousand worn old tramp steamers carrying England's poor far from her shores. Still she said nothing.

Things improved when Charlotte and Louisa found their cabin. Though small, it was clean and had two sets of bunk beds. A floral china wash basin and water pitcher stood on a painted wooden stand, and Louisa commented on their pretty design. She was over her initial anxiety and excitedly pulled Charlotte outside to see their names on the cabin door. The visiting card read, "Miss Charlotte Townsend," and below it "Miss Louisa Townsend."

"Oh Lottie, we may be the only women on board with a visiting card." Impressed, she went inside and tried sitting and lying down on each lower bunk, several times. Charlotte remained outside. Farther down the rail she noticed a woman about the same age as herself. She was tall, gaunt and pale. Though a part of the huddled group sponsored by the Columbia Emigration Society, she, too, was standing alone and looking at the grey-green shore through the drizzle. She turned and for a moment their eyes met. Charlotte would remember that hollow face for a very long time.

"What an odd assortment they all are," Charlotte said to her sister as she came inside. "I'm so glad Papa bought us our own cabin." Charlotte sat on the edge of her bunk, thinking of the group of which she and Louisa had become a part. Many were female orphans, barely teenagers, rescued from the London slums, and cramped six and eight to a cabin. From the sound of their laughter, the accommodations and the adventure that lay before them, the voyage itself, was a gift from heaven. Charlotte looked at Louisa, then glanced at herself in the small mirror and for a moment, she was jealous of their youth.

Charlotte felt uncomfortable with the fact that she and her sister, as paying passengers, would be subject to the demands and restrictions of the chaperones employed by the Columbia Mission Society to watch over the group of lively teenagers. However, Papa had insisted they not travel alone and they had relented. Charlotte anticipated that the chaperones would accept their education, class and age, and not treat them as schoolgirls. She was anxious to meet them and offer her assistance with the younger girls, gaining, she hoped, a degree of independence.

All that afternoon the tender ferried small groups of passengers out to the steamer. Louisa darted nervously up and down the rail, and commented on all the comings and goings to her sister. She watched, too, the blackened, burly men who seemed to be continually moving coal about the ship. Charlotte had noticed that the women from the Columbia Emigration Society filled most of the row of cabins just behind the ship's funnel. The other women like themselves, who had paid for their own passage, occupied the remainder of the cabins in the row. The last two cabins were each designated with a visiting card. The first one read, "Mrs. Robb, Matron, Columbia Emigration Society." The last one read, "Reverend Scott, Columbia Mission Society." Charlotte became concerned when she saw an officer cordon off the area around the cabins where all the single women would be housed, but assumed it was simply to reserve for them a common area of deck space.

Farther aft, behind the mizzenmast, was another group of second-class cabins. She watched as ship's officers scurried in and out of them with newspapers and small bags. Later that afternoon, Charlotte saw one literary-looking gentleman carrying books and an easel into one of these cabins. Soon after that, Louisa came running; she excitedly told her sister that two handsome young men had smiled at her as they entered their own cabin.

The artist was Frederick Whymper. His upper-class parents were well-known English water-colourists who had exhibited at the Royal Academy. Well travelled and well taught by his parents, Frederick had been listed in the Royal Academy of Arts at 21. Capitalizing on the many European countries the family had visited, he had co-authored and illustrated several travel books with his father and brother. Now, as a gentleman sojourner of 24, he was off alone on his greatest adventure. He would sketch the goldfields of British Columbia and travel and paint in Alaska. Whymper was going to Canada to do a book. He would keep a journal, full of his adventures and sketches, and publish it upon his return to England. If he saw Louisa and her sister, he didn't acknowledge it.

The two other gentlemen that Louisa saw were third-class passengers Charles E. Redfern, a jeweller from London, and Edward Coleman, also an artist and amateur naturalist. Unlike Whymper, they were immigrants and were going to British Columbia for a better life, drawn by the stories of promise they had heard from the goldfields.

By evening, low clouds scudded across the harbour. The black waves in the roadstead crested silver in the falling light, and it grew cold. Louisa and Charlotte had taken the air long enough and were tired of wandering around the small, enclosed deck that seemed to have been roped off from the rest of the ship. Their cabin, though comfortable, was confining. Charlotte found a dining room of sorts that served paying passengers and the two sisters decided to peek in. They might meet one of the smartly dressed ship's officers, who could reserve a small table for them. But a stout woman in black suddenly appeared and told them that they would eat, at least this evening, in their cabin. She would arrange for sandwiches and tea to be sent round. Just as suddenly, she disappeared. It had been a long and worrisome day for Louisa and Charlotte so they didn't object, though Charlotte thought to herself that if Papa were here they would eat where they pleased. Later, in her bunk, Charlotte wondered if the woman was the matron. She felt the cold steel of the bulkhead beside her, and sensed that Louisa, too, lay wide-awake. Soon she heard the driving rain and felt the motion and swing of the ship. Sleep was fitful.

Successful though shipping magnates William Lindsay and Miles Stringer were, they knew that competition for the emigrant trade was fierce. Windjammers such as the *Frigate Bird* offered ocean passages that were almost as fast as steamship travel, and had a record for safety that the steamships could not yet match. Older sailing ships such as the *Romulus* or the *Dawn of Hope,* full-rigged ships less renowned than the clippers, offered steerage rates to Australia for less than Lindsay's fare to British Columbia. Cunard Line's side-wheel steamers easily outclassed the *Tynemouth*, and offered first-class passengers cuisine fit for royalty, shipboard entertainment and a private promenade deck. Passage to America on Carman and Pearce's *City of Boston* included connecting tickets with the Grand Trunk Railway, while the Cariboo Line had a whole fleet of fast packet ships, such as the *Ashmore, San Francisco* and *Bendixen,* that sailed directly from Liverpool to Victoria. More, the *Bendixen* carried only first-class passengers and had a reputation for fine service. Its cabin fare for the passage was only £50. Charles and Robert Green each paid £42 for less favourable third-class accommodation on the *Tynemouth*. Lindsay and Stringer bet on the hope that its passengers didn't scan the papers for the best deal, and prayed that steerage would be filled to overflowing with wretched emigrants who would make up the slack. A voyage on the *Tynemouth*, even with her new engines, was not a good deal.

This was Captain Hellyer's first merchant command. He had been hired as master of the *Tynemouth* moments before the ad for the voyage had appeared in the London *Times*. At 46, Alfred Hellyer had been trained in the Royal Navy and was certified as a ship's master in 1851. Like many of his kind without a command, he bided his time as an officer in the Royal Navy Reserves. When Lindsay and Co. told him the ship would sail with less than a full complement of crew, it took him some time to figure out that it was more a measure of economy than a shortage of trained seamen. Hellyer would not discover the consequences of this decision of the owners until too late.

To an officer used to protocol and Royal Navy spit and polish, the *Tynemouth* crew seemed sullen and undisciplined. He noticed his officers, their pea jackets open, loafing at the rail and eyeing the women. Things would have to change. The voyage of the *Tynemouth* was going to test Hellyer's mettle to the extreme.

By the beginning of June 1862, the *Tynemouth* had a complement of 292 passengers, mostly steerage and third-class emigrants, who occupied the bowels and forepart of the ship, while the few second-class passengers were, according to tradition, placed in cabins aft. Sixty of the passengers were single women sponsored either by Maria Rye's agency or by the Columbia Emigration Society. The two groups were essentially seen as one and would be overseen by the Columbia Mission Society's chaperone and padre.

The sponsored single women were quartered amidships in Spartan, third-class "staterooms" as they were euphemistically called. Each cabin had berths for six. Charles Redfern noted that the space was indeed very small. He stated that there was just "enough standing-room to allow the occupants to dress and undress, unless they all wished to do it at the same time."[3] Just behind the belching funnel was a deck area cluttered with ventilators, ship's boats, coils of line and standing and running rigging as well as the quarters of the women for the duration of the voyage. The bulkheads between the cabins were clammy and rusting, and when the air temperature dropped at night, condensation turned into rivulets of water which ran down into the bunks. Rheumatic aches, resulting from sleeping in the wet, were suffered in silence.

Young single miners and gentlemen travellers alike, all heading for the goldfields of British Columbia, would be attracted to 60 single women on a ship like iron filings to a magnet. Knowing this, the Columbia Mission Society took drastic steps to ensure that the women dressed and undressed without any male companions. The first line of defense against any shipboard philandering was to be the Anglican missionary, Reverend William Richard Scott.

Reverend Scott of St. Mary Magdalen Church, Harlow, had signed up for missionary service to help convert the natives of the Sandwich Islands. Like John Sheepshanks or Lundin Brown before him, William Scott had been caught up in mid-century missionary zeal and was eager to spread the gospel to the heathen aboriginal. However, Scott was considered by many in the Columbia Mission Society to be very High Church, quite severe and somewhat emotional. When he applied for service, the society's governors thought he would not easily adapt, and he was therefore felt not to be a particularly good candidate. However, missionary societies needed people and Scott qualified. He had intended to sail to the islands in the summer of 1862 with the Reverend Thomas Nettleship Staley, the newly consecrated Bishop of Honolulu, but the Columbia Mission Society asked Mr. Scott at the last minute if he would oversee the sponsored women, and sail to Victoria instead. He could leave, he was assured, for Honolulu from San Francisco at a later date. Eager to be seen as tractable, Scott agreed. With his wife, Harriet, as superintendent and his two daughters in tow, William Scott boarded the *Tynemouth* just as she was about to depart. The London *Guardian*, newspaper of the Anglican Church, was most pleased with the appointment and reported favourably:

> When the various temptations and evils of any emigrant ship are considered, we may be thankful for the sake of the Columbian Mission that Mr. and Mrs. Scott have undertaken the important task of caring for their special passengers, and that they will have on the voyage not only

pastoral help and privileges, but the presence of a lady educated and refined who will be always ready to help and advise. We may also be glad that the Bishop has secured a man with heart and courage to undertake a voyage so unexpectedly; it augurs well for his future work in those interesting islands.[4]

The *Guardian* would be forced to eat its words.

The educated and refined woman chaperone was Mrs. Robb, the woman who had subtly but firmly insisted the Townsend sisters eat alone in their cabin that first evening. Uncompromising and strong, Isabella Robb and William Scott made the perfect pair. The Columbia Mission Society was pleased to offer Isabella a contract, for she was a nurse who wished to emigrate but could not afford the fare for her family and goods. As matron on the *Tynemouth* to "sixty marriageable lassies," Mrs. Robb would be allowed to bring along her husband, James, a son, James Jr., and two young daughters, Jane and Jessie. Mrs. Robb would further be granted a liberal baggage allowance, and she had brought along the family's English feather bed, a chest of drawers, a china tea set, two brass candlesticks, various pewter pots and trunks of clothes. Together, the zealous padre and the possession-laden chaperone would make the shipboard lives of the women in their charge utterly miserable.

The first passenger steamer to travel from Britain to British Columbia, the *Tynemouth* left the Dartmouth roadstead on the morning tide of June 9, 1862. As she entered the western approaches of the English Channel, she sailed smack into a southeast gale. All hell broke loose. A cow that had been tied in a makeshift stall on deck was thrown about, maimed and washed over the side. This was a serious loss as many passengers, and especially their children, now had no milk. Several pigs were also kept on deck, but under the cover of the forecastle. They were slammed against the steel bulkheads. Bloodied, with broken bones, they squealed hysterically until they, too, were washed overboard. The fury of the gale increased and Frederick Whymper noted the deteriorating conditions of the passengers:

> On board were some three hundred passengers, two thirds of whom showed a total loss of dignity and self-respect during those early days, and made our vessel much resemble a floating hospital.[5]

Louisa Townsend became very seasick, so ill that Captain Hellyer had her moved from her cabin to special quarters nearer amidships to lessen the motion. He was initially nervous toward his paying passengers, and did not want any negative publicity on his first trip. For a week Louisa could not eat and she became seriously dehydrated; the captain was afraid she might die.

The passengers in steerage received no such attention from the captain or any other of the ship's officers, but Hellyer's attentions to Louisa did reveal his professionalism, albeit toward his own class. The same humanitarian impulses had not been felt by Captain Wyman on board the *Seaman's Bride*.

Charlotte was beside herself. Hellyer had a special, more delicate diet prepared for Louisa so she might begin to eat, and Dr. Chipp, the *Tynemouth* surgeon, and other officers took turns watching over her; Charlotte remained by her bedside for two weeks.

The storm itself was never a threat for the stoutly built *Tynemouth* and she resolutely nosed her way southward beyond the Bay of Biscay and the Azores, into the calmer waters of the mid-Atlantic. It was, however, an early, unnerving prelude of more serious things to come. As the weather warmed and Louisa returned to health, she and Charlotte began to understand something of the rules of shipboard life that they had accepted in travelling under the protection of the Columbia Mission Society.

On any voyage of over three months, such as the slow, westward trek of the *Tynemouth,* only the few second-class passengers had any sort of shipboard freedom. Often Charlotte saw Frederick Whymper, writing or sketching, or smoking a cigar in a lounge chair on the afterdeck. It was an area of the ship they were not allowed to enter, not because they were not of the same class, but because of the ever-present and watchful eyes of the chaperones. Charlotte was resentful until she understood that conditions in steerage were much worse than what she had to put up with herself.

Passengers in cabins represented only a very small part of the total shipboard population, yet they alone had access to most of the vessel's more inviting, more livable spaces. People in steerage were jammed into windowless quarters well below decks. Charlotte hardly ever saw any of them on the main deck and became cross with a blushing young seaman who told her that the blackened hatch covers and ventilators would be opened for them only in fair weather.

Passengers in steerage, if they were not controlled, could pose a very real threat to the security of a vessel. Captain Hellyer and his officers knew this, as did those who ran the company. Discontent over the conditions of shipboard confinement, should they deteriorate, could instantly turn passengers' frustrations into mob action. The look of the women from steerage, when Charlotte occasionally saw their sick faces at the rail, told her that storms were felt more severely below. She wondered how such a group could remain so compliant for so long.

The reason that emigrants in steerage didn't turn rebellious over their appalling conditions was a system of shipboard social control that was both ingenious and cunning. Building on the rigid English class system and the ingrained submissiveness of generations of the working poor, order was maintained on an emigrant ship by a variation of the game of "Divide and Conquer." The agency of that division was the distribution of food. Steerage passengers and those travelling third class were not served food prepared by a chef, as were those who ate in the ship's dining room. They were given a portion of daily rations, and under a self-regulating, mess system of small groups, they were simply left to fend for themselves.

A particular passenger, usually a male, was given the responsibility of being the mess-captain of a small group of individuals. It would be his task to have the daily rations collected from the ship's quartermaster and then prepared and cooked by those he designated within his group. The success of the meal became a function of the compatibility of the group. Limited cooking utensils and scarce fire-boxes meant that what was used had to be cleaned and readied for the next mess. Messes that did not pull together, or were slovenly and unclean, not only ate poorly, they suffered the wrath of another group, impatient to use the utensils and begin its own preparations. Discontent was controlled through the urge to satisfy hunger, a primary need.

One group was played off against another. Through the mess system every able person in steerage was given a task that contributed to the welfare of a small group. Many hands were kept busy preparing the all-important meals of the day. If the buckets in the head were not emptied, those responsible did not eat. There was no time for revolution.

The mess system also enabled the ship-owners to make extra profit. Wages for ships' cooks or stewards were not required, and provisions could be of poorer quality because the meal's success was the responsibility of a particular mess-group. Steerage passengers were encouraged to bring extra condiments, such as pepper or sauce, relieving owners of further expense. The quartermaster was also allowed to sell any provisions left over at the end of a voyage, and his profit depended on the miserly distribution of the low-grade rations. Dissatisfaction and aggression were turned inward and, like the concentration camps of the 20th century, self-regulation was the key.

Charles Frederick Green and his brother, Robert, travelled third class on the *Tynemouth*. Their passenger contract stipulated the dietary rations they would receive during the 99-day voyage:

In addition to any Provisions which the Passengers may themselves bring, the following Quantities, at least, of Water and Provisions (to be issued daily), will be supplied by the Master of the Ship, as required by Law, *viz.*, to each Statute Adult Three Quarts of Water daily; and a Weekly Allowance of Provisions, according to the following scale:

5¼ lb. Biscuit, 6 oz. Suet, 6 oz. Butter.

1 lb. Preserved Meat, ½ lb. Raisins and Currants, 2 oz. Salt.

½ lb. Soup and Bouillon, 2/3 pint Peas, ½ oz. Mustard.

1 lb. Mess Pork, ½ lb. Preserved Potato, ¼ oz. Pepper.

1½ lb. India Beef, ½ lb. Rice, 1 gill Vinegar.

½ lb. Preserved and Salt Fish, 1 lb. Raw Sugar, 1 gill pickles.

2 lb. Flour, 1¾ oz. Tea, 6 oz. Lime-juice.

1 lb. Oatmeal, 2½ oz. Coffee, 21 Quarts Water.

When Fresh Beef is issued, 1 lb. To each Adult per day will be allowed; there will be no Flour, Rice, Raisins, Peas, Suet, or Vinegar, during the issue of Fresh Meat. 1lb. Of fresh Potatoes may be substituted for ¼ lb. Preserved Potatoes.[6]

Charles Redfern later recalled the social organization that he and the women from London endured for three long months:

> Meals were not prepared and served to us as is customary now [in 1922] with third-class passengers. Periodically rations were served out to a representative from each cabin for the number of occupants, which rations had to be prepared. [Once prepared] for cooking by the recipients, [the food was] taken to a large galley on the forecastle and delivered to the cook, whose duty it was to attend to the same and supply hot water for tea, coffee, or for drinking purposes.[7]

The "cook" was not a cook; he was simply a member of the *Tynemouth*'s crew who kept order in the galley. Any rations such as oatmeal porridge, which required constant stirring, "the passenger had to attend to himself."[8] Redfern also noted that the *Tynemouth* had no condensers for the production of fresh water, so plates, cutlery and cooking utensils were all washed by the passengers in buckets of cold seawater. Food poisoning was never far away.

Clothing washed in seawater soon became caked with salt and even on fair-weather days, after having been hung out to dry in the wind, it remained damp. Without fresh water for rinsing, a body washed in seawater was prone to the inevitable salt-water boils. After months at sea, the difficulty of personal grooming caused many people to give up on washing altogether.

Despite all this, young Charles Redfern counted his blessings. He felt himself lucky in that his small cabin was occupied by only three other young men. Mercifully, two empty bunks provided extra room for storage. Up to a point, the deck was his to wander. He could buy stale lemons and bad cigars from "Old Mo," a venerable Jewish merchant who had also decided to emigrate and was hawking his goods to other passengers long before he opened his shop in Victoria. Redfern was free to make the acquaintance of others of his station from all over England, all bound for the same exciting, unknown colony. If he were careful, he might even find a place on deck for a quick nip of whiskey that his new friends had brought along. Talk, inevitably, would turn to the group of single women.

Here, under the eagle eyes of the Reverend Scott and Mrs. Robb, their young and not-so-young charges were watched over as if imprisoned. Though free to roam within the small, cordoned-off deck space, the women were not permitted to go beyond the makeshift rope barriers that Charlotte had seen rigged before the vessel left England. More, they were forbidden to talk to other passengers, especially the young men. At best, they could catch only a glimpse of the raffles and mock auctions organized farther down the deck by Old Mo, or attempt a discreet wave at a dashing young man smoking at the rail in the distance. When Old Mo intoned his heavily accented "highestch prishe for old closhe and zhewellry,"[9] they would have sighed, crestfallen, and returned to peeling potatoes, airing mattresses and washing clothes.

Rations were handed to Mrs. Robb. Under her supervision, the girls did the cutting and initial preparation of the meals in large pots. At the barricade, Mrs. Robb could have co-opted any number of eager young gentlemen to carry and stir the victuals in the *Tynemouth's* forward galley, if only to catch a single longer look at the girls. Mrs. Robb was determined, however, that no *man* was ever going to enter *her* cloister! For the girls themselves, the only male voice of any significance that they heard for a goodly part of the trip was the droning, pontificating outpourings of Reverend Scott, who was known to prostrate himself on the deck at Communion.[10]

As others, Frederick Whymper noticed the women trapped in their shipboard corral, and commented on their situation:

> Our most noticeable living freight was, however, an "invoice" of sixty young ladies, destined for the colonial and matrimonial market. They had been sent out by a home society, under the watchful care of a clergyman and matron; and they must have passed the dreariest three months of their existence on board, for they were isolated from the rest of the passengers, and could only look on the fun and amusements in which every one else could take a part.[11]

Whymper didn't agree with the mandate of the "home society" that sponsored the women and as an upper-class conservative, he believed such ventures should best be left to the forces of the marketplace:

> Every benevolent effort deserves respect; but, from personal observation, I can not honestly recommend such a mode of supplying the demands of a colony. Of course much might be said about giving the poor creatures a chance! But the fact is that the market would, in the course of affairs, more naturally supply itself. The prosperous settler would send for his sweetheart, or come home in search for one, and could always get suitable domestics sent out by his friends, and meet them at the port of arrival.[12]

Whymper also had a very moral view of the women:

> It will be readily understood too, that in a new country there is a floating population, among whom some

individuals by "chance" or by industry have acquired a little money, and are ready to plunge into matrimony on the slightest provocation; while there is also a large proportion of "black sheep" who are quite ready to amuse themselves at the expense of the poor girls.[13]

The demands made of the *Tynemouth*'s crew were even more severe than those of the organizers of the mess in steerage. Worst off were the coal-haulers and the stokers. To feed the engines, haulers physically moved tons of coal 24 hours a day, from the hold in the fore-deck to the bunkers aft. Low pay, poor diet and accommodations no better than those in steerage made many seamen rebel or desert at the first opportunity. Working a sailing vessel was hard enough for any young strong back, but sail-handling *and* hauling coal besides was something else. The rough breed of men that took to the sea in ships throughout the 19th century could, if ill treated, create a storm of protest more threatening to a skipper than any natural typhoon. In the Royal Navy, such protest would be met with the whole force of the Admiralty; on a sloppy, dilapidated tramp steamer such as the *Tynemouth,* in a poorly managed merchant service, it could spell disaster.

It happened one Sunday morning, well into the voyage and some time after the first bout of rough weather.

"Charlotte, the engines have stopped." Louisa nudged her sister from her sleep. Charlotte opened her eyes and lay very still.

It was true. The incessant though reassuring throbbing of the engines was gone. The ship rose and fell silently, drifting aimlessly on a glassy sea in the middle of the South Atlantic. Considerably overworked, several stokers and haulers had left their stations and let the boiler fires die. The *Tynemouth,* sails flapping idly, was dead in the water. The ship was in the middle of a mutiny.[14]

Together the Townsend sisters left their cabin and walked beyond their barricaded deck space. Charles Redfern, coming toward them, told them what had happened. The coal-haulers, with some sympathy from the rest of the crew, had refused to work extra duty. Sensing that the unrest had not spread throughout the entire crew, and believing that the balance of power still lay with his loyal officers, Captain Hellyer, in the tradition of the Royal Navy, had swiftly rounded up the insurgents and thrown them into a makeshift brig. He charged them with mutiny on the high seas and told them that they would be kept manacled and in confinement until such time as they might answer to the charges against them. For the moment all seemed well.

However, the detainment of the offending crewmembers posed a dilemma for Captain Hellyer. Without men to fuel the engines, caught in the windless doldrums near the equator, the *Tynemouth* would soon become a scorched spectre-ship as in the *Rhyme of the Ancient Mariner.* The bride-ship women now crowded the rails of their deck space, and steerage passengers milled about on the main deck. Hellyer assembled all able male hands and issued an ultimatum. He said that unless the passengers themselves replaced the coal-haulers and kept the boilers fired until they reached the coaling station in the Falklands, the *Tynemouth* would have to return to England, under sail alone, to find replacement crew.

An undercurrent of alarm spread throughout the whole ship. They had come this far and survived, and no one, not even those in steerage, wanted to go home. Whymper scribbled feverishly in his diary:

> At this juncture a committee of passengers was convened, and it was agreed that the more active of all classes should

be invited to volunteer, and act as crew for the time being. All the younger men came forward readily, were solemnly enrolled, and set to work at once, glad of an interruption to the monotony of the voyage. We scrubbed the decks, hauled at ropes, filled the coal-sacks, and hoisted them on deck, getting a fair taste of a modern sailor's life.[15]

Whymper, the aristocrat, saw the affair in patriotic terms. For him, unused to hard labour, it was jolly good fun: the landed gentry, dirtied and bare-chested, fighting with the proletariat for England and the Empire. He burst into poetry:

It is more than doubtful whether any of us would have echoed the words of England's sea-song writer, who says, "Then Bill, let us thank Providence That you and I are sailors!" But we found it good exercise and worked with a will.[16]

The dapper and elegant Whymper knew that the game was really about sporting in front of the ladies, and his view of them had altered slightly due to the attention that they now paid to him:

Did we not know that the eyes of sixty maidens were looking on approvingly as we helped them on to the consummation of their dearest wishes? We did, and even our parson creditably proved his "muscular Christianity," and soiled his irreproachable garments at one and the same time.[17]

So Charles Redfern from third class, along with his cabin mate Edward Coleman, ended up working beside the renowned painter,

Frederick Whymper, and the Reverend William Scott. The girls loved it and under their admiring gaze the broad-shouldered young men endlessly filled and moved the unwieldy sacks of coal from one end of the ship to the other. Redfern enjoyed the attention, but he enjoyed something else more:

> I think we rather enjoyed the fun of it; especially as at the
> end of each day's work we were munificently rewarded by
> the gift of a pint bottle of stout, and what we prized above
> all things, plenty of fresh water to wash with. Some of us, as
> we could not get a bath, used to get up early in the morning
> when the sailors were washing the decks and get them to
> turn the hose on us, which they always did, to their great
> glee and our satisfaction.[18]

Captain Hellyer's tough action against the rebellious crew seemed vindicated. Order had been restored, the boilers were being stoked again and an amicable relationship had sprung up between some seamen who were not involved in the protest and many of the working passengers. The *Tynemouth* steamed on toward the distant Falkland Islands and more coal. For almost a month things seemed settled, but the peace did not last.

One morning as Whymper was in the middle of breakfast, he heard a commotion on deck and saw Charlotte, Louisa and many others race by a dining-room porthole. Whymper was on his feet, napkin still in his hand. He rushed out and joined the throng. What he saw stopped him dead in his tracks. Several angry crewmembers had grabbed Captain Hellyer, along with some of his officers, and had them pushed backwards over the edge of the stern rail. The sailors were screaming blasphemies, shouting recriminations, raising clenched fists and calling for blood.

Horrified, the Reverend Scott and Mrs. Robb were trying to herd their charges back to their compound but to no avail.

The *Tynemouth* was suffering another mutiny and this one was decidedly more violent. Captain Hellyer's entreaties were lost in the din. Suddenly, an enormous black seaman, undaunted by the officers' uniforms, stepped forward and faced the captain. Then, with one mighty blow, he struck Captain Hellyer squarely in the face. This time, the bloodied skipper did not have the upper hand and in an instant the mutinous crew were ripping officers' clothes, bashing their heads and drawing blood. Above the uproar of the brawl, Captain Hellyer shouted for the officers of the deck to "Put them in irons!" But it did no good. The undisciplined merchant officers were frozen with fear. Clearly the captain, in the grip of the deranged African, was about to be tossed over the side. Many of the younger girls, who had refused to budge for Mrs. Robb earlier, now ran screaming to their cabins. The Reverend Scott was right behind them, praying out loud, fearing what the mutineers might do next.

In another instant the handful of passengers who were drawn to the stern by all the noise plunged into the fight; then and only then were other ship's officers stirred into action. A phalanx of belaying pins appeared and the mutineers were beaten off. Soon they were manacled where they lay on the deck. Another uprising had been put down, but only just in the nick of time. Captain Hellyer, bleeding and clearly ruffled, regained his composure. He ordered the prisoners to be dragged away and placed in a small, hot chamber right beside the engines. There, he said, until they reached the Falklands, the idea of open revolt would be sweated out of the marrow of their very bones.

In all, 16 sailors from two attempted mutinies had been placed under arrest. In a vessel undermanned from the start, the further loss of manpower was disastrous. Keen young civilians stoking boilers was one thing, but the *Tynemouth* didn't have enough coal to steam all the way to the Falklands. It had been Hellyer's original intent, once the ship was in the southeast trade winds of the South Atlantic, to work his vessel slowly toward the distant coaling station. Now, short of experienced crew, that plan evaporated.

The task of sailing a 1,500-ton, full-rigged ship in the boisterous winds, with three masts and acres of sails that had to be furled and unfurled on spars hundreds of feet above the deck, was no job for untrained passengers, however strong. Without real sailors, the *Tynemouth* could never sail home. Without coal, the ship would never reach Port Stanley. Captain Hellyer, in a clean shirt and tie, walked the deck reassuring the passengers that all was well again. To Charlotte and Louisa, whom he had come to know, he tried not to show his worry.

What saved the ship were two things. Among the passengers there were some who, in the past, had gone to sea. They knew the business of a sailing ship, the code of the forecastle, the power of a team. They could tell at a glance the difference between a clewline and a buntline, and how to brace in a yard. Now, for their very survival, they, along with the remaining loyal crewmembers, would train others to remember the names of a thousand lines and man-haul them, instantly when necessary, to bend on the topgallants, set the gaff-topsails, heave the braces, keep a watch and steer a course. They would sail the *Tynemouth* themselves to a small dot on a chart at the very edge of the world. The other blessing was that the trade winds, that July of 1862, were for the moment, fair.

The former sailors and conscripted landlubbers became so good at their appointed tasks that the *Tynemouth* soon made nearly 100 miles a day under sail alone, but after a week or so of this there was a decided change in the smell of the air. They were south of the estuary of the River Plate, beyond Montevideo, at about 38 degrees south latitude, and 60 degrees west longitude, and fast approaching a region with weather completely different from that of the trade winds. Here, winds unencumbered by any land rage around the bottom of the world to be squeezed between the continents of Antarctica and South America. Here, the Southern Ocean began to send the *Tynemouth* the first of its infamous undulations, the merciless Cape Horn swell. Some said it was a bad omen.

Spin-off winds from the "Roaring Forties" often shoot up the coast of South America, bringing with them storms of killer renown, and the *Tynemouth* sailed into one just days after her neophyte crew had learned the lines. It began around sundown.

Hellyer's more experienced sailors raced aloft to take in sail, while others ran to the main deck to tie down the hatches and clamp shut all the portholes. Oil lamps were secured and all fires extinguished. Steerage passengers were ordered to their bunks in the darkened dormitories below. There, families hugged each other and children cried as the noise of the waves boomed the length of the hull. In the cloistered cabins of the women, shoes, mugs, chairs, clothing and sea chests careened and clattered mercilessly as the vessel rolled nearly to her beam-ends. The Townsend sisters in one bunk held each other tightly, while nearby, other women shrieked as every hammering wave vibrated throughout the ship. Young men lay awake, wide-eyed with fear. Nature would now take its course.

Darkness fell as the wind increased from gale force to hurricane, and the *Tynemouth* lurched and heaved and shuddered to the seas. Great torrents of water surged up and down the main deck like the raging current of a river in flood. With every bolt of lightning, the few officers around the helm saw frozen, skeletal-white images of a group of seamen who had secured the lifeboats and taken refuge in the forecastle. As the ship fell off seas 50 and 60 feet high, she charged down the troughs and threatened to keep going to the very bottom of the ocean. Then, she would suddenly slow, almost bursting her rivets, only to rise to the onslaught of more waves and begin the process anew. As she pitched, the open forecastle flooded, and the men tied loosely to a capstan were washed about like flotsam in a wreck. One face streamed with blood.

At the height of the storm the *Tynemouth's* main deck was continuously awash with swirling ocean that the scuppers could not handle. The men on the bridge thought the vessel would founder. Captain Hellyer had a seaman repeatedly blow two short blasts on the ship's foghorn to summon all hands trapped forward to the safety of the higher deck. Many of the crew simply did not understand the signal. Yet instinctively, when they felt a lull, one or two attached themselves to a jack-line with a shackle and ran pell-mell to a ladder. Only the phosphorescence of the crashing seas and the flashes of lightning illuminated the scene.

Suddenly, a rogue wave crashed against the side of the ship. The *Tynemouth* rolled, hung and slowly recovered. But a rail around the deck had given in to the seas and a precious lifeboat was gone. Just as suddenly an ominous rumbling sound began in the bowels of the ship; some empty iron tanks had broken loose from their lashings deep in the hold. Beneath them the far more dangerous freight of bound stacks of long, thin railway lines strained at their harnesses. Throughout the night as the *Tynemouth* plunged, shivered and rose to the seas, the empty tanks smashed back and forth across the rails, slamming into the sides of the hull.

Reverend Scott believed the apocalypse had come and prayed with his wife and children. Louisa, her head in Charlotte's arms, moaned, "We're going to die; we're going to die." Had the railway lines broken free and punctured the hull, the *Tynemouth* would have disappeared without a trace.

Near dawn the winds and seas abated. They had not lost a mast, been swamped by following seas, nor turned broadsides and rolled over. Again the *Tynemouth* had survived. Later in the day, one by one, cabin portholes were opened to the gray and eerie light. Pale and sickened with terror, passengers and crew alike crept gingerly out onto the deck. Other than the loss of bulwarks and a ship's boat, the *Tynemouth* was intact. The fires were lit again, the injured were bandaged and hot tea, savoured in tin cups, calmed frayed nerves. Many people from steerage came up to the main deck, lay down and slept. No one bothered them. The girls from the cabins on the half-deck simply sat outside and watched an albatross wheel amidst the scudding clouds. Talk was hushed.

Southward, with sails again unfurled, the ship continued beyond Bahia Blanca and Puerto Descado. The *Tynemouth* inched its way down a chart across the parallel of 50 degrees south latitude. In time, as the days wore on and the skies cleared, the seaworthy vessel and her young novitiates gave each other renewed confidence. Once more, to the joys of the porpoises, they roared on. A thin yellow band of cloud far ahead made some believe in the possibility of land. Yet, with only days to go, the tight little ship again caught the whiff of death.

Throughout the mutinies and furious storms the women had endured. Now, the break in the weather was treated as a godsend, even though the luxury of a fresh-water wash was, because of limited tankage, still out of the question. Many just sat, talked, sewed and soaked up the blessed sun. However, poor food, the lack of sanitation, the damp, the confinement and constant fear, had done its work. Miss Rye's women and those of the Columbia

Mission now faced a problem that rivalled all that fate, so far, had thrown their way. The sunshine, the endless blue skies and the mesmerizing lifting and falling of the rolling green seas seemed not to matter. One of their own was desperately ill.

Elizabeth Buchanan had taken to her bunk. She had been sick, feverish and fretful for two days. It was as if Charlotte's fear for her sister, earlier in the voyage, now gripped everyone; she saw it in their faces. This time, however, the symptoms were different. The Reverend Scott prayed. The *Tynemouth*'s surgeon, Dr. John Chipp, who had helped Louisa, could do little, except demand complete isolation and cold compresses. Maria Duren, possibly one of the orphan girls from the London slums, offered to help Dr. Chipp. She had seen much sickness before and instinctively cooled and soothed Elizabeth's brow. Dr. Chipp was glad of the help, but thought Maria was at risk. Often the two glanced at each other. Both watched fearfully for the appearance of the disfiguring blisters — the telling sign that Elizabeth had caught the dreaded smallpox. They did not come.

Two days before reaching the Falkland Islands, Elizabeth died. Smallpox was never confirmed, but it was never completely ruled out. She would be buried in an alien land that she had never seen. Her grave was in a cemetery in Port Stanley among others who had died on the seas; it would be cared for by a lightkeeper's wife and visited only by a few wandering sailors. Her name and her hopes would hardly be mentioned again. Charlotte, alone in the night, remembered a hollow face and wept.

Elizabeth Buchanan had died, but the fearsome shipboard epidemic did not come. As they neared land, other passengers smelled the bite of kelp and saw shadowed hills so green they cried. The *Tynemouth*, strong as ever, minus one, rounded Cape Pembroke. They had made the Falklands.

They stayed 13 days, and what a stay it was. For some, after six weeks at sea, land, any land, seemed like heaven. For others, the arrival was the cruelest cut of all. The Reverend Scott and Mrs. Robb decided that since there were ships and their crews in the anchorage, the women in their charge would be safer if they remained on board. Considering the experiences all had suffered in getting to the Falklands, the harshness of the chaperones' decision cannot be understated. For six weeks, the Columbia Mission women had been confined to a deck space of little more than 50 feet. Now, with long trails beckoning among the green hills, ice-cold fresh-water streams to dabble in and the residents of Port Stanley to engage in boundless conversations, the women could only watch others of the *Tynemouth* indulge in much-needed rest and recreation. It is a wonder that the women, having witnessed two insurrections on board the ship, didn't now mount one of their own.

Though the snow had retreated from the lowlands, the midwinter winds were still so strong in the harbour that for several days, Captain Hellyer did not allow the remaining longboat to leave the lee side of his vessel. On those days, *everyone* gazed longingly at the land. When the wind finally abated and the excited passengers again scrambled into the waiting boat, the absurdity of the moral stance taken by Mrs. Robb and the Reverend Scott must have been palpable. It was not by any means the last cruelty or indignity the women would suffer at the hands of those charged with their care.

For those who did make it to shore, it was sheer bliss. In August the southern winter was coming to an end, and the lowlands bloomed. The meadows above Port Stanley were a velvet rug of green, cut by elongated patches of black peat moss that ran in lines to watery bogs. The smell of the open earth, the ozone from the life-giving peat, fuel for the islanders, blew across the anchorage. On shore, ship-weary passengers pointed and laughed in amazement at the hundreds of cattle that roamed wild and free on the hillsides.

Port Stanley would have seemed, even to those from London, a most exotic place. Everywhere was the stamp of British colonialism, something most had never before seen. Though at the time it had only 700 or 800 inhabitants, there was a church, a school, government buildings, a barracks and stores with fresh meat and provisions. Everything was diminished in size to be sure, but familiar and new at the same time. The passengers ashore luxuriated in milk and eggs and fresh vegetables, then hiked for miles to stretch legs that had almost forgotten how to walk.

In the land-locked basin was the comforting presence of ships from China, Australia and California. Some were there for coal; all were there for water and for healing. A Royal Navy warship, part of the Pacific Squadron at Valparaiso, flew the White Ensign. On the hill a Union Jack strained against the breeze. Frederick Whymper and his friends went shooting wildfowl, then enjoyed the antics of penguins.

At the Cape Pembroke lighthouse, eight miles east of town, they climbed the steps and saw the 18 oil lamps that illuminated the rotating mirror and focussed its narrow beam of light a mere 14 miles out into the darkness. At the edge of the sea cliffs, on a bright and windy afternoon, they stood and looked far and long out to sea. Then they talked to the lightkeeper's wife, and learned that her brood of young children had never ventured even to Port Stanley, but did not seem to mind.

Back in town, Whymper and others with money had discovered a treasure trove even more invigorating than the walks, the welcome or the good green earth:

Port Stanley was a free port at the date of our visit, and our passengers took advantage of the fact to lay in stocks of Holland's and brandy, much to the disgust of our steward, who firmly believed in monopoly.[19]

Meanwhile, on the anchorage, officers and crew of the *Tynemouth* with shore leave who were sympathetic to the plight of the women brought them back soap, milk, eggs and oranges. Frustrated and angry, the women could only glare at the matron; some even refused the shipboard chapel. From below they heard the clamour of the mutineers who were screaming blue bloody murder from the confines of the brig. Captain Hellyer had the Royal Navy come over and give them a talking-to. In the merchant marine, they were still alive; in the Royal Navy, they were told, they would have been strung up or shot. All went quiet.

When the 16 men were brought ashore to the courthouse for trial, Hellyer showed great foresight. For the rounding of Cape Horn still to come, the captain knew the *Tynemouth* would need seasoned crew, so he testified that he thought their confinement was "sufficient punishment for their insubordination and that he would be willing to take them on board if they would promise to do their work for the remainder of the voyage without giving any further trouble."[20] The majority of the mutineers agreed to Hellyer's terms. The most vociferous, and most violent, did not. They were incarcerated in the British garrison ashore and received a term of imprisonment with hard labour. The hard labour consisted of keeping the garden and sanding the floors of the government buildings around Port Stanley. Some of the officers scoffed at the light sentence, but Captain Hellyer didn't. Being incarcerated on the Falklands doing busywork was, for a sailor, a fate worse than death, yet Hellyer knew he was giving the miscreants another chance. Other vessels would soon arrive in port short-handed, and their captains would offer the prisoners who had served their sentences wages that were higher than what they had received from the miserly owners of the *Tynemouth*. Hellyer, the Royal Navy man, had been shrewd; he had rid himself of the worst of the men and they, by virtue of future opportunities, would not hold a grudge against him. Unfortunately, the crewmembers who gave their word of loyalty to him and returned to the ship were not to be trusted.

It was crisp, clear and cold on the day the *Tynemouth* left the Falklands for the last, month-long leg of its voyage to British Columbia. Frederick Whymper had discovered that "the captain of the warship offered to pilot our ship through the Straits of Magellan, but our captain could not accept the offer as his ship was insured for the voyage round Cape Horn."[21] More likely, Hellyer was making a statement about the command of his vessel. He was not going to give up his ship to anyone, and that included mutineers and his peers in the Royal Navy, who were often contemptuous of those in the merchant service. Hellyer now felt he could take on anything, and that included the seas of Cape Horn.

It was a piece of cake. The sea was so flat at the bottom of the world that Captain Hellyer steered the *Tynemouth* in close to the cape so his passengers could get an eyeful of that "bleak and inhospitable"[22] mythic promontory. The peaceful conditions at the moment were a blessing, but they would soon turn out to be a curse.

When Frederick Whymper and some third-class passengers shot wildfowl on the Falklands, it was not for sport; it was serious business. The fresh poultry would prevent the return to the dreaded ship's rations en route to San Francisco. So many dead birds were brought back on board that a section of the ship took on the appearance of a country market. Many of the gentlemen smoked cigars they had bought in town, while farther down the deck the women from the London slums happily plucked and cleaned the birds. The plan was that the birds, once eviscerated, would keep for a week or ten days hung out in the cold weather of the Southern Ocean. It was Christmas in August and for days, cabin passengers, and even some of those in steerage, gorged themselves on duck soup, goose breast and drumsticks and perhaps even a little home-made stuffing, sharpened with the tang of fresh onions.

It ended abruptly just four days later when an officer was sent among them. With instructions from the captain he was "to see that every bird left was thrown overboard."[23] The cause of Elizabeth Buchanan's death was not clear; she could have died from smallpox or typhoid fever, but she might also have died of food poisoning from months-old bully beef. Now Captain Hellyer and Dr. Chipp were taking no chances with aging fowl. Fresh as they still appeared to be, the birds were jettisoned. The indignant cries of the angry passengers were drowned out only by the calls of ravenous gulls.

Once the ship was around the Horn, the Pacific Ocean refused to co-operate. It remained passive and calm when there ought to have been wind. For hundreds of miles the *Tynemouth* was forced to steam north through the calm, undulating swells when she should have been able to sail. The coal supply was running out, and tacking against the prevailing winds, if and when they came, would take weeks. The fires in the ship's boilers, starved for fuel, flickered "to the last gasp."[24] A week before they arrived in San Francisco, Captain Hellyer ordered all loose wood on deck, including the deckchairs, boxes for life-preservers, notice boards, and even some valuable extra spars, thrown into the insatiable furnaces, just to keep the vessel moving through the slumbering seas. On the day before the *Tynemouth* reached San

Francisco, "it was seriously contemplated to strip the second and third [class] cabins of their berths and furniture."[25]

When the *Tynemouth* reached the Falklands, it had been a deliverance. When the steamer finally made San Francisco, it was a mixed blessing. She stayed only two days, just long enough to take on coal. It was time enough, however, for 34 male passengers to leave the ship and check into various hotels for a hot bath and clean sheets. A fine bottle of claret and a meal prepared by a real chef was the treat for those who could afford to pay. Reverend Scott and Mrs. Robb had decided that the time in port was too long for unescorted ladies to be alone in the city, so they called for yet another shipboard detention of their female charges. As the tender, full of shore-bound passengers, left the vessel the women seethed with indignation. Two days was long enough for almost half of the *Tynemouth*'s remaining crew to desert the ship completely. *The San Francisco Herald* failed to notice the rats leaving the still-floating ship, but they did notice the damsels on deck:

> Colonization of British Columbia — The steamship Tynemouth has on board some twenty unmarried female emigrants, whose intention it is to settle in British Columbia. Their rosy cheeks and *embonpoint* [stoutness] show that they will be valuable accessions to the Colony. We learn that another vessel is on the way with 500 other British beauties on board who seek the same destination. Victoria will shortly have attractions for the young men of California, of which that city has not hitherto been able to boast.[26]

The news raced up the coast and was published in the Victoria *British Colonist* just hours before the *Tynemouth* reached the Esquimalt anchorage. Rumour and memory made the news sensational:

> How many manly hearts will beat with pleasure as this paragraph reaches their eyes, we dare not think; but we are sure that pleasurable emotions will pervade every bachelor heart in this "great" metropolis when we state that the good steamer Tynemouth with sixty select bundles of crinolines, arrived at San Francisco on the 10th inst., and was to sail in a few days for this port with her precious freight — that is, if the Yankees don't steal their affections during the few days the vessel may lie at that port — as was the case with the Seaman's Bride female passengers.[27]

The *British Colonist* was proud to announce that an Immigration Committee had made all the arrangements for housing the women upon their arrival at the Marine Barracks in Victoria. Applications from families requiring domestics, the paper noted, should be registered with the committee as soon as possible.

When the *Tynemouth* steamed out of San Francisco on September 12, 1862, she did so in a hurry. Several passengers bound for Victoria had misinterpreted the time of embarkation, and Captain Hellyer, already frustrated with the seamen who had deserted, simply left them on the wharf staring in disbelief. As the *Tynemouth* departed the bay, Hellyer's troubles, even on this last leg, continued. With the number of crew who had jumped ship, the *Tynemouth* was again drastically short-handed. The crew who had remained loyal were given extra duty and protested vehemently, some even refusing to work altogether. Captain Hellyer was growing weary of the on-going labour disputes and this time he took the initiative. Four of the most vocal protesters were arrested, charged with mutiny on the spot and thrown immediately into the brig.

After 99 days at sea, the unhappy little ship finally reached its destination. With one death, three mutinies and a group of women who had been confined for three months on board, as if they were in prison, all was not well. Captain Hellyer faced a lawsuit from the disgruntled passengers who were left in San Francisco, while several crewmembers faced jail for their actions against the Laws of the Sea.

The Townsend sisters never did get the chance to wine and dine with gentlemen travellers on board, and thoughtful Charlotte still suffered over the death of Elizabeth Buchanan. Ironically, many of the women brought to Victoria with the promise of a better life faced even more "protective" incarceration. The whole hellish trip was enough to make Louisa Townsend say she was sorry that she had ever come.

Chapter Six
THE ARRIVAL OF THE *TYNEMOUTH*

GOOD NEWS! — The Girls Have Arrived! —and A. J.
Brunn has reduced the price of his well-selected stock of
fashionable clothing, shirts, hats, caps, and furnishing
goods. See advertisement![1]

The Fraser River and Cariboo gold rushes made
Victoria, for a time, a boomtown. With so many
single men still in the city, the promise of a shipload of
eligible maidens created quite a stir. When it became known that
the girls hadn't been kidnapped in San Francisco by damn Yankees,
and with rumours abounding that more were not far behind, the
editors of the local press turned natural jubilation into patriotic
pandemonium. By September 11, the *British Colonist* had firmly
set the tone:

The "Tynemouth's" Invoice of Young Ladies
A general holiday should be proclaimed; all the bunting
waved from flagstaffs; salutes fired from Beacon Hill;

clean shirts and suits of good clothes brought into
requisition, and every preparation made to give this precious
"invoice" a warm welcome.[2]

Victoria in 1862 was not blessed with many respectable single
women. The few "good" women there were, were the wives or
daughters of the English colonial officials who ran the place. For a
small businessman or miner who wanted to settle down and raise
a family, access to the daughters of the landed gentry was almost
impossible as such families tended to move in closed social circles.
To gain entry, a potential suitor had to be an officer in the Royal
Navy, an up-and-coming civil servant, or a gentleman with
connections. The only other available females in town were
prostitutes or aboriginals, and for men who wanted a socially
acceptable permanent spouse, neither option was promising. For
the respectable single man in Victoria in 1862, there was not much
to do except join a church or a temperance union. One other, less
demanding distraction, was to attend the theatre.

In the days immediately before the first bride-ship arrived, the
theatrical impresarios in the city paraded a veritable cornucopia of
sweet young things in front of some desperately lonely men. Night
after night, the theatres were full as Clara Dean and other music-
hall stars beguiled their all-male audiences with the popular,
romantic airs of the period. When some ended their performances
with a round of "fancy dancing"[3] thrown in for good measure, the
places went wild. The press, like the bachelors, also fell in love
with the showgirls, and when Belle Divine sang light opera, it was
reported that she "filled the house with sweetness."[4] When it was
revealed that Colonel Moody was so taken by actress Lulu Sweet
that he promptly named an island at the mouth of the Fraser River
after her, tickets for her performance in *The Maniac Lover* were

simply not to be had. Against such sweet diversions, organized religion had a tough row to hoe.

By the second week of September many a bachelor's heart had been stirred. For those who missed the thespians' charms directly, they could, at least, read and dream of them through the newspapers. Ever the strategist in promoting his newspaper, *British Colonist* editor Amor De Cosmos toyed with his readership. On the day that the notice of a lawsuit against the *Seaman's Bride* first appeared, and on the same page as a review of Belle Divine, the wily editor further tantalized his male readers with a story of women's undergarments:

> Ladies' Dresses in 1809 — I remember the time when no young woman who went "into the world" ever appeared till she had tied on *before* a semi-circular cushion of a quarter of a yard long and wide, and two inches thick. How we could have been such fools, is to me amazing; or how we supported that horrid composition of calico, and horse-hair in crowded assemblies in the dog-days; or how we reconciled it to our feeling of cleanliness to wear one of those machines till we were tired of its form, without washing, appears now beyond my belief. This fashion ... has been without a parallel in false taste and absurdity since that period.[5]

If Victoria's young dandies had been set to thinking of flimsily dressed dancers on stage, and even more provocative and revealing women off, the girls on the *Tynemouth* couldn't have arrived at a worse time. The showgirls on stage were unattainable; the ladies in their imagined underwear were unmentionable: the *Tynemouth* girls were a fact.

The *Tynemouth* arrived at 8 o'clock on the evening of Wednesday, September 17, 1862, and anchored off Esquimalt for the night. News of her arrival had preceded her by only two or three days, and everyone — the press, merchants and the welcoming committee included — was left scrambling for information. There were only rumours, but they were enough. With a suspected boatload of marriageable English lasses eagerly waiting to come ashore, what man could resist buying, at least, a new studded collar, and racing to the waterfront for a closer look at a real woman?

A few excited young men, who could contain themselves no longer, simply had to be the first to see this miracle for themselves. However, Captain Hellyer had asked, through port officials, for the executive council to place a police officer on board immediately to watch over the four most recent mutineers that he had thrown into the brig. The request was granted and Officer Douglas was dispatched. He would also keep a close eye on the restless women who, until the plans for their immediate care in Victoria were known, were being held on board ship an extra 24 hours. Passengers not travelling under the aegis of the Columbia Emigration Society were allowed to disembark immediately.

Four randy bachelors and a married philanderer had somehow learned of the presence of a police constable on board, and thought they should not attempt to sneak onto the vessel under cover of darkness. The sleek silhouette of the *Tynemouth,* with its white anchor light high in the jack-stay, and its flickering lights from cabins amidships, would have tantalized the young men bent on intrigue, but the "rosy-cheeked English beauties"[6] and their keystone constable were not interrupted that first night. The five adventurers were patient, as well as clever, and they would execute their exploit in the full light of the following day.

Their plan was as simple as it was bold and right out of *Romeo and Juliet*. They had learned that the vessel would be overrun with welcoming dignitaries most of the next day, so they would simply don suitable disguises and "crash the party." Once aboard, disguised as members of the press or the clergy, they could easily mix and get the first long eyeful of the women who could, conceivably, become attached to their lives. Their mates ashore would be full of glee and disbelief when they learned of this venture. It almost worked.

By mid-morning preparations were complete. One put his noose-collar on backwards to imitate that of a cleric. The others shined their boots and donned starched white shirts; their garroted collars were each affixed with a new pin. With pencils and notepad, two would pass as reporters. Two others, with the addition of a perfumed handkerchief in the breast pockets of their morning coats, would become high-ranking civil servants. They gave each other final nods of satisfaction and with grins held in check, the hopeful five set out in a hired longboat across Esquimalt Lagoon. In the distance the *Tynemouth* rode peaceably on her anchor, though already there was much activity on her deck.

On board, representatives of the welcoming party were milling around and chatting about the changes that a boatload of female governesses and domestic servants would make upon their fair community. When each was sure that no one else was watching, the good gentlemen of Victoria cast long glances at the better-looking young women. For the most part the women weren't paying attention. However, it didn't take long for some of the younger girls to notice the five well-dressed young spiffs fast approaching in an open boat. Excited, they began to giggle and move to the ship's rail to wave and get a better look. The gentlemen on board were uncertain of the identity of the approaching men of obvious good breeding, and one was perturbed enough by the attention they were getting to have himself a bit of fun. Pointing to the nearing longboat, he put on a dour disposition and asked Captain Hellyer if he knew any of the gentlemen on board. The captain's negative response prompted the wag to respond, "You'd better look out for them."[7]

Captain Hellyer, by now more vigilant then ever, became immediately concerned. The *Colonist* ran the full story:

"What do you mean?" asked the captain.

"Nothing, nothing, only you'd better keep an eye on those fellows, that's all."

The captain looked puzzled and glanced at his informant doubtingly.

"Yes," continued the latter, vaguely, assuming a sanctimonious air and tone of voice. "Take my advice, sir, and keep them off."

"Do I understand you, sir," said the captain, "that the respectable looking men in that boat are not to be trusted among these females?"

"Most certainly they are not; why (pointing to the oldest man in the party, who is the father of a large family) that steady looking old gent is the worst man in the crowd."

"Are you quite sure of the truth of what you say, sir; that gentleman looks like a minister — and I *shouldn't* like to offend a minister."

"A minister! Yes; he does look like a minister; but that air is assumed that he may better consummate his designs. They are none of them to be trusted aboard this vessel, or anywhere else where there are innocent females, I assure you, captain."[8]

Captain Hellyer's reported response was exceedingly naïve: "Is it possible that such depravity exists in so young a colony?"[9]

Hellyer, however, became convinced of the joker's story and ordered the five in the longboat away. The captain then asked Officer Douglas to enforce his order. The longboat, now so close, lay dead in the water and the five, fearing detection, could not even look up to meet the eyes of the excited young ladies. Other women at the rail soon began to voice their disappointment that the skiff of handsome young men might be turned back. Some gentlemen on board, ignorant of the joke, joined the protestations. Captain Hellyer, convinced that those in the longboat might indeed be interlopers, stepped to the rail to support the command he had given his constable, "notwithstanding the entreaties, expostulations, and protestations of 'honorable intentions' from the whole [on board] crowd."[10]

Crestfallen, the five intruders, fearing their disguises would land them in even more mischief, turned and rowed slowly away. On board the *Tynemouth* the practical joker, who had outdone those in the skiff, slipped away among the officials. The other invited guests soon returned to their small talk and their undetected ogling of the women, whenever the opportunity presented itself. The would-be boarders, like pirates, had been repelled.

It is not known whether or not Amor De Cosmos was the on-board perpetrator of the comments that had turned the hopeful dandies away, but it would not be surprising, given the journalistic scoop that was at stake. What is known is that the next morning, Friday, September 19, the *British Colonist* printed the first eyewitness description of the long-awaited women:

Arrival of the "Tynemouth" — As a matter of course, we went aboard the steamer yesterday morning and had a good

look at the lady passengers. They are mostly cleanly, well-
built, pretty looking young women — ages varying from
fourteen to an uncertain figure; a few are young widows who
have seen better days. Most appear to have been well raised and
generally they seem a superior lot to the women usually met
with on emigrant vessels. Taken together, we are highly pleased
with the appearance of the "invoice," and believe that they will
give a good account of themselves in whatever station of life
they may be called to fill — even if they marry lucky
bachelor miners in the Cariboo. They will be brought to
Victoria and quartered in the Marine Barracks, James Bay,
early this morning by the gunboat *Forward*.[11]

Along with that information, De Cosmos made passing mention
of some trouble with the crew on the way out, but felt it was
"nothing very serious." Obviously, his interest was somewhere else.

On the same day, De Cosmos chose to reprint a long letter he
had received from "our London correspondent" nearly a full year
before. Dated August 2, 1861, the correspondent revealed news
of a fund-raising benefit in London's Exeter Hall in aid of
Britain's Female Middle-Class Emigration Society. The
correspondent reported that Exeter Hall middle-class was full
to overflowing and most supportive of the society's aims. De
Cosmos wanted it known that the colony of Vancouver Island
should share in the "reflex benefits"[12] that female emigration would
have on those living in and around Victoria. In fact, the London
letter was a call for local money:

Female emigration schemes more especially call for our
immediate attention. The main body of the sufferers in
consequence of the stoppage of the supply of cotton are

females — married and unmarried. They constitute a large proportion of the hands employed in the factories. Even those who are married earn their own living and help to support the young members of the family by daily labor in the Lancashire hives of industry. Young women form the staple of the craft.

Until recently the Central Committee of Relief was established in London and the rich men in Manchester at first pooh poohed the statements regarding the distress and seemed to look upon foreign interference as a matter of impertinence. They have, however, I am glad to state, been shamed into action in this matter.

Her Gracious Majesty ... has come forward and contributed £2000 ... £5000 have been sent from India, and sums varying in amount will no doubt come in due time from British Columbia. Vancouver Island will unquestionably not be behind in this work of mercy.[13]

Though Victoria already had an immigration board, the activity of the Columbia Mission Society in Britain earlier that spring had prompted certain citizens, including Commander Verney, to consider the formation of an appropriate committee to serve the special needs of females who came to the colony. They named themselves the Victoria Female Immigration Committee and initially, did little except talk. They agreed that its mandate was not to raise money for far-away England, but to oversee in the manner of "noblesse oblige" the mission girls' safe arrival in their city. The Female Immigration Committee consisted of two parts; a men's group whose job it was to announce the arrival of the women and plan the official welcome, and a women's group, which was to arrange for the girls' welfare once they were landed.

The men on the committee were some of Victoria's most prominent citizens. Among them were Lieutenant Commander Verney of the Royal Navy gunboat HMS *Grappler,* J. A. Grahame, Chief Immigration Officer, Gilbert Sproat, manager of Anderson and Co., exporters of spars (masts) to Europe from Puget Sound and Vancouver Island, Robert Burnaby, President of the Chamber of Commerce, the Reverend Edward Cridge, Anglican minister of Christ Church Cathedral, Dr. W. F. Tolmie, former Chief Factor of the Hudson's Bay Company in Victoria, and soon-to-be member of the Legislative Assembly, Dr. J. C. Davie, apothecary and secretary of the committee and Archdeacon Wright of the Anglican Diocese of Victoria. The shipboard gathering, which was well under way the morning the gate-crashers made their attempt, was arranged by this body.

Once the eagerly awaited girls arrived, the women's committee would set to work placing them in local positions. The ladies who served in this capacity were members of the Anglican Church in Victoria and attended, in the main, Christ Church Cathedral. The women's committee included such distinguished members as Mrs. James Douglas, wife of the governor, Mrs. Thomas Harris, wife of the mayor and Mrs. Edward Cridge, wife of Reverend Cridge. Lesser notables included Mrs. Joseph Trutch, Mrs. Arthur Fellows, Mrs. Mowatt, Mrs. Alston, Mrs. Rhodes, Mrs. Nagle, Mrs. McCreight and Mrs. Woods.

Unfortunately, Victoria's Female Immigration Committee was strictly an ad hoc group that had neither the blessing nor the sanction of members of the government. The *Tynemouth* women were landed while Vancouver Island's civil authorities were away. James Douglas, the governor of the colony, was on the mainland, George Hills, the Anglican bishop, was in the Cariboo, and Archdeacon Wright was in New Westminster. The committee's plans were hampered because officially, it didn't exist; hence, it received no information from London that the *Tynemouth* was even under way, and news of its departure became known only through the press. Verney's estimated, but inaccurate, time of arrival of the ship in the middle of October had lulled the committee into inactivity, so no concrete preparations had been made when the stout little vessel hove into view a month early. Verney wrote to his father, "You will divine how aghast the committee looked, when they were told that their sixty young ladies might be expected in two days or less."[14]

Suddenly, the first bride-ship had arrived, and nobody, save the journalists, knew anything about it. The so-called committee, fielding inquiries from interested Victoria families who wished a domestic servant or governess, didn't even have a list of the women on board, never mind their occupational background. In the scramble for information, it was discovered that a semi-official list had, in fact, been sent to Archdeacon Wright's office, and two committee members were allowed to make a copy in private. The committee had no idea how to respond to questions regarding the wages employers might have to pay the girls, nor did they know if London would provide any compensatory funding for the girls should they require immediate accommodation.

In the panic, the women's committee suddenly lost three of its members. One left because she had decided to go, for a period, up-country. Another had on-going appearances in court and a third unexpectedly announced that she had "important business,"[15] and would not be able to serve. Those who were left raced to prepare for the girls' imminent disembarkation. Hastily, the men's committee determined that a public announcement regarding the girls' availability for domestic service or tutoring was of paramount importance. On the spot they recommended to prospective employers that an annual wage of £25 was sufficient for the girls and that an extra processing fee should be paid in hard cash to the committee to cement any negotiations. The notice was placed in the Victoria *Daily Press*:

Arrival of the "Tynemouth."
Persons desiring GOVERNESSES or SERVANTS are requested To apply in writing to Mr. Graham at the Immigration Office, corner of Fort and Broughton streets, stating the description of service needed, and the rate of wages offered. Fee payable to Office on engagement of a servant to be $10.
By order of the committee.
J. C. Davie, Hon. Sec.[16]

In the meantime, the women determined that temporary accommodation could be secured for the *Tynemouth* girls in the vacated Marine Barracks near the Legislative Buildings. However, nothing was known of the condition of the buildings, and resources, if required to make them ready for occupancy, were non-existent. That aside, the women's committee all agreed that until they were able to find suitable situations for the girls in homes around the city, they should, for their own safety, be confined in the barracks under strict lock and key.[17]

This last concern was not entirely unfounded. The publicity surrounding the girls' arrival had been so played up by the press that many single men in Victoria had fallen prey to the sensationalism. The High Church women wanted to be sure the girls were properly chaperoned, while the Royal Navy, through Commander Verney, wanted to put on a show. With the best of intentions, what these special interest groups would soon achieve was a most despotic control over the girls' lives, and, ironically, a most curious disorder. Collectively, they ensured that the *Tynemouth* women would be treated ashore first like monkeys in a circus and then like convicts in a cage. Together, they created a spectacle that would attract the whole city.

The Daily Press was a short-lived newspaper in Victoria, and its editor, like Amor De Cosmos of the *British Colonist*, hated the ruling aristocracy. Mischievously, the editors of the *Press* placed the following notice in their paper on the day that the bride-ship women were scheduled to disembark:

Landing ex. "Lockett,"
10 HHDS. DEMERARA RUM, 30 o.p.
10 hhds. Hennessy's and Martell's Brandy
10 Qr. Casks Port
10 " " Sherry
60 pkgs. Bass No. 3 Ale, in bulk ...
All of which are offered at low prices.
E. STAMP & CO. Wharf street.[18]

The Daily Press had given notice that if the English ruling class was going to take undisputed control over the *Tynemouth* women, then the ordinary miners from the interior creeks or the local saloons were going to be able to attend the welcoming festivities well lubricated.

Friday, September 19, was "cold but delightfully fine."[19] After 106 days of continual confinement, the women from the first bride-ship were finally coming ashore — only to be confined some more. Despite the hardships they had all suffered en route, the prospect of leaving each other caused six of the girls to become hysterical. Two of them fainted with grief on the *Tynemouth*'s main deck.

Little did they know that what awaited them ashore was only slightly better than the desperate experience they had endured on the voyage.

The Royal Navy gunboat HMS *Forward* was dispatched to the *Tynemouth* at three o'clock Friday afternoon to ferry the women from the anchorage in Esquimalt Lagoon into Victoria proper. Lieutenant Charles Robson made sure the warship was all spit-and-polish for the short, three-mile trip. Since local businesses had decided to close for the day, the disembarkation of the bride-ship women was fast becoming an occasion.

Charles Hayward witnessed the goings-on. He was a young carpenter who had recently arrived in Victoria and was, for a time, busily engaged in digging a well for Dr. Davie of the Immigration Committee. Hayward noted in his diary that there was "much excitement in town owing to [the] girls arrival."[20] The actual time and place of their landing was kept from the general public for as long as possible. Yet, as soon as it became known that they were being landed from a Royal Navy gunboat, people guessed correctly that the landing would be at the small wharf at the inner end of James Bay. Upon that information, Hayward noted, "a continuous stream of humanity set in towards the point, which very shortly resulted in every inch of ground from which a view could be obtained being occupied by men of all ages and colors."[21] The garish "Birdcages," the nearly completed new Legislative Buildings, just above the water, aptly topped the scene as the spectacle of the women's arrival began.

As the *Forward* steamed slowly up the inner harbour, the vessels it passed whistled and dipped their colours. The men lining the shore doffed their hats and cheered. "Hundreds of prospective grooms had flocked to Victoria from throughout the colony."[22] In Victoria itself, "a large and anxious crowd of breeches-wearing bipeds"[23] joined them along with children, dogs and worried mothers with a few curious teenage daughters held firmly by their side. Reports estimated that a crowd of 300 gawking and shoving people gathered on the beach near where the gunboat's tender would land. As the *Forward* entered the inner harbour and steamed round the last bend, spontaneous clapping, laughter and even more cheers filled the air. Just in case hormones got the better of decorum, city authorities had strategically placed four Victoria constables and four Royal Marines on the wharf to ensure that order would prevail.

Two girls were to be spared the humiliation of what was to follow, because of some upper-class interference. An English feminist, Louisa Twinning, a member of the London Female Middle-Class Emigration Society and a friend of its founder, Maria Rye, was a cousin of Mary Moody, the wife of Colonel Richard Moody, Commander of the Royal Engineers in New Westminster. Through her cousin, Mary had written to the London society requesting domestic help for her five children. Maria Rye granted Mrs. Moody's request and two of the orphans were earmarked for her. On the day the young women of the *Tynemouth* were being brought to the wharf in James Bay, two were immediately transferred to the paddle-wheeler *Enterprise,* for the trip across the Gulf of Georgia to New Westminster. Six other girls followed the first two to the mainland colony days later.

Back on shore, the spectators pressed closer to the water as the *Forward* rounded up in front of the Birdcages and dropped anchor. More cheers arose as a few girls at a time climbed down a makeshift ladder into the longboat. Suddenly they were ashore. One of them moved to the edge of the wooden planks of the small wharf, knelt down and scooped up a handful of moist, dark earth. As the longboat returned to the *Forward* for another load, the girls were directed to line up, in schoolgirl fashion in twos, and walk up from the harbour toward the Legislative Buildings. The way had been cleared for them and cordoned off by more Royal Marines and Victoria bluejackets. Several uniformed officials, keeping the ogling crowd back, led the way. The short corridor up from the beach, instead of being a ceremonial pathway, as Commander Verney of the committee had envisaged, had now become a gauntlet.

Many of the girls were still dressed in the clothes they had worn on the ship. Most had little else. They were dirty, tired and nervous and certainly did not look their best. Some probably suffered from borderline malnutrition; all suffered from an acute lack of exercise. The orderly line created by the men on both sides did not last, as the men in front, pushed in by those behind, struggled to keep from falling or being shoved into the women. The girls who could, ran; the older women and those frightened into straggling, were inspected even more closely, amidst hoots and cheers from all sides. Some of the girls, who had had enough of shipboard confinement or were perhaps angry at Reverend Scott and Mrs. Robb for their continued confinement, found alcohol. Now that they had arrived it didn't matter, they thought, what the chaperones decreed. Commander Verney, who was on hand for the occasion, noted that "one female was carried up helplessly intoxicated, and two or three more were *evidently* the worse for liquor."[24]

Along the noisy corridor one young London orphan got the shock of her life. Up until then, miners, miscreants and merchants had all jostled with each other on both sides of the narrow route to secure the best location to eye the girls as they passed by. Young Sophia Shaw did not know that she was being watched right from the outset.

Sophia had caught the attention of "Mr. Poineer, a Cariboo miner."[25] He had been successful on the diggings and had walked many days to be in the crowd that morning. Suddenly, before the police could act, he stepped out in front of her and proposed on the spot. Taken aback, young Sophia was speechless. The young man then reportedly drew out $2,000 in cash from his pocket, gave it to her and told her that if she accepted him, she should buy clothes for the wedding. The crowd nearby drew in its collective breath and hushed. Strangers whispered to each other; all anxiously waited for Sophia to respond. Her shipboard friends drew up about her. Sophia recovered and looked at the young man for what seemed a long time. She looked at the money that he had placed in her hand and looked at him again. Time stopped. Then Sophia smiled at the tired, unkempt prospector who held tightly onto his simple cap with both hands, and put the money away in her dirty apron. The crowd roared.

Commander Verney missed the proposal, but he wrote home detailing the events of the wedding. "Everything was ordered to be carried out in tip-top style: the milliner was instructed that the bridal dress was not to cost less than £400; the breakfast not less than £200: a ball took place in the evening, at which the bridegroom became tipsy: the next morning, he came back into the ballroom to see if his wife was still there, as he had not seen her since supper."[26] Commander Verney had not heard whether Sophia had turned up or not. He thought that "she was a smart, flashy girl, but not without some good in her."[27] He did report, however, that the wedding bash was certainly a night to remember. Not all the women from the bride-ships would find such good fortune so soon.

In front of the Legislative Buildings, "great tubs of water, hot and cold, and plenty of soap had been placed in readiness in case we had linen that we wished to wash at once."[28] Many of the orphan girls sponsored by the Columbia Emigration Society did not hesitate to publicly wash their linen, their arms, their necks and even their hair in the soft, fresh, hot water. Others, more shy, watched and smiled as water, soap and laughter flew about. Louisa and Charlotte Townsend looked on. They had worn their oldest clothes aboard the *Tynemouth*. When she had anchored in Esquimalt Lagoon, the two had pushed their dirty clothes through a porthole. "We arrived in new garments with trunks full of lovely things."[29] Most of the other girls weren't so well supplied.

Fifty-nine women had come ashore, "and nearly half were received into people's houses at once."[30] The New Westminster *British Columbian* noted the majority as "slender, having the appearance of girls from 12 to 15 years of age."[31] The Columbia Mission Society had sponsored girls from St. Margaret's Home in Grinstead, as well as others, probably from Angela Burdett Coutts's Urania Cottage in London. Soon after their arrival, the Victoria Female Immigration Committee interviewed several of the foundlings. Typically, one of them said, "I don't care where I goes, or what I does, so long as I gets plenty of money."[32] The older women, those educated gentlewomen travelling with the Columbia Emigration Society under the aegis of the London Female Middle-Class Emigration Society, less certain or eager to marry, hoped to become the governesses that Victoria did not really need. When the committee questioned one of these women, her response was as extraordinary as that of the waif. "I really cannot undertake anything like hard work; I should like an American family where I should be on a footing of equality."[33] Though indeed their moneyed upbringing had given them a different set of social expectations, the educated gentlewomen were treated ashore as they were on board the *Tynemouth*, their class and status ignored completely.

From the legislature the women, still followed by the crowd, were escorted to the Marine Barracks. The barracks were part of a complex of seven government buildings on the same property as the new Legislative Buildings. The barracks would be moved to the naval base in Esquimalt, but for now they were immediately behind the building where the girls had just washed.

Soon after the very public scrubbing, the women's committee divided the bride-ship girls into three groups. The younger children were placed in homes as domestics, until they were old enough to marry. The single girls 15 and up would be offered immediately as brides, and housed at the barracks until they had been proposed to, or found work. The older women — the widows and teachers and governesses — would also be granted temporary residence in the barracks until appropriate employment could be found for them.

Having discovered the barracks in a terrible state of disrepair, Commander Verney instructed the crew of HMS *Grappler* to scrub and clean the place. By Friday noon, just hours before the girls were to be landed, the tradesmen had finished their renovations and all was ready. However, in the melee of the morning's activities, the committee had forgotten the more immediate needs of the girls. After a morning during which most of the bride-ship women had not eaten because of nerves, common courtesy demanded that they should have been offered a cup of tea and a bite when they could, at last, sit down. However, there was no food or kitchen equipment in the barracks.

In this instance it wasn't the women's committee that stepped into the breach; it was, again, the enlisted men of the Royal Navy. John Marshall was a gunner on board HMS *Grappler*. Feeling sympathetic toward the girls' plight he decided to take matters into his own hands. Marshall raised money from his shipmates and borrowed necessary utensils from neighbouring residents. He may also have raided the *Grappler*'s own stores. Marshall then raced into town and purchased food from a grocer. He bought pots from a hardware store and instructed the proprietor to send the bill to the women's committee. Careful not to get himself court-marshalled for his unorthodox actions, Marshall made a point of borrowing a teapot from the wife of Corporal Bowman of the Royal Marines.

The Daily Press publicly commended Marshall for his action and made him the hero of the hour. The gunner deflected the acclaim with great aplomb by responding to the *Press*'s approbation with a letter to the paper's editor. Marshall wrote that he had:

> acted entirely under the direction of Commander Verney, as one of the Immigration Committee. At the same time, it affords me pleasure if, by promptitude in exercising such orders, I have been enabled in some slightest degree to add to their comfort in their new home.[34]

The editors of the *Press* responded by clearing Verney's committee with a disclaimer:

> The above explanation from Mr. Marshall speaks for itself; and we are informed that the necessity for procuring utensils, &c., was created by the outfit so liberally furnished by the Immigration Society not being available at the time of debarcation.[35]

However, the *Press*, still disdaining the gentry, criticized the women's committee for its lack of attention to the needs of the girls as they arrived at the Marine Barracks. The situation showed outright "mismanagement" and it was lack of "duty," reported the newspaper, that the immediate "wants of arrivals be imposed upon naval officers in such an unlooked for manner."[36]

Though the committee was praised for its zeal in finding suitable servant situations for the girls, it was also soundly condemned for manipulating the service contract in favour of certain well-heeled Victoria employers. It was known that the committee had set the wages to be paid to a girl in household service at £25 a year. The *Press* charged that the committee had been able to lower these wages by sending more than one girl to a single household, and several households in the city were accused of taking advantage of this change to the detriment of the girls' own welfare. The *Press* wrote that the committee worked "to the object of keeping down the price of wages by combination [rather] than doing their best in their power for the benefit of their charges."[37]

On the day after the girls were installed in the barracks, the Royal Navy held its annual regatta, and Commander Verney suggested that they spend the day on board the *Grappler* to participate in the festivities as guests of the navy. Genuinely concerned for their welfare, Verney was, as others, taken by them. He wrote to his father:

> Some of the little ones are very pretty, and attractive: I do not know whether this is quite grammar, but I am talking of the immigrants: I think the little orphans from East Grinstead took my fancy the most: perhaps that is because, being only twelve, they do not expect to get married at once.[38]

With many of the older girls on board his own ship, Verney was able to loosen up a bit. While his ship's company won rowing prizes in the longboats, the girls were "regaled with buns, sherry, tea, & etc. The committee were ex officio at this point and entitled to a more recherche [*sic*] repast a la fore sheet in the captain's cabin,"[39] and no doubt a little alcohol made him bolder in conversation with a few of the girls he admired. Verney obviously liked the company of the young women, and had an opportunity to observe them closely. He noted:

> one or two of the women are *thoroughly bad* and must have been so before leaving England, and there must be unpardonable neglect somewhere that they were ever allowed on board [the *Tynemouth*].[40]

He had clearly watched some of the girls interact with crewmembers, and was able to distinguish girlish guile from hardened sexuality.

Morality was also one thing that the Female Immigration Committee took very seriously. On Sunday, September 21, some 30 of the *Tynemouth* women were sent to their first Church of England service in the New World, in Christ Church Cathedral. The Reverend Scott, the prostrate padre who had accompanied the women on the voyage, would be preaching the sermon. Verney knew that "Mr. Scott was not popular with some of the females,"[41] and that Captain Hellyer and Scott had not spoken to each other since the *Tynemouth* had arrived in the Falkland Islands. Verney liked Hellyer, and though he didn't say it directly, he had some doubts about the treatment the girls had received under Scott's care. It didn't take long for Bishop Hills to uncover the bad feelings between William Scott and his charges, yet he wrote in his journal only that the women "objected to being restrained."[42] Nonetheless, Reverend Scott stood proud in the pulpit that morning, restraining his girls yet again. He exhorted them to:

> remember their religious duties and the duties to their employers, always and under any circumstances to shape their conduct so that they might prove a credit to their

English mothers, from whom many were now separated forever; and when beset by sin and temptation to rely on kind Providence for aid and comfort.[43]

The pontificating padre then turned his fire on the would-be employers of the young women. He reminded the upper-class women of Victoria that they had an equal obligation to their new servants. Scott "besought them to look well to the precious charge which had been placed in their keeping."[44] The *Colonist* reported that Scott's eloquence, in the best High Church mid-Victorian tradition, caused many women in the congregation to weep, though it failed to report the probable straight faces of those from the *Tynemouth*. Charles Hayward didn't succumb to tears, but he too was most impressed by Scott's sermon. He remembered the minister's closing blessing, and noted it in his diary: the Reverend Scott was full of joy, "hoping they would soon be comfortable as English wives and mothers."[45]

Throughout the sermon, the girls were compelled to sit bolt upright and control their restlessness; some looked at each other and rolled their eyes as Scott droned on and on. The girls were not the only ones who regarded their padre with disdain and suspicion. Lady Jane Franklin, widow of Sir John Franklin, the lost Arctic explorer, was also suspicious of the Reverend Scott's religious rhetoric and strange demeanour. She had been in Victoria briefly the year before.

At that time, Lady Franklin visited her old friend Captain George H. Richards, who was stationed with the Hydrographic Survey of the Royal Navy in Esquimalt. Richards was then commander of the steam sloop HMS *Plumper,* though he had been part of the Edward Belcher expedition that had searched the Arctic in vain for signs of Franklin's *Erebus* and *Terror* in 1852. More importantly,

Lady Franklin had been asked by Angela Burdett Coutts to visit
Bishop George Hills and report on the progress of the Anglican
Church in the colony. The *Colonist* was most impressed with Lady
Franklin, and considered her tour of inspection "a most singular
mission for a lady."[46]

As emissary for Angela Burdett Coutts, Lady Franklin was well
chosen. Like Miss Burdett Coutts, she was both a fervent Christian
with the zeal and energy of a missionary and a loyal supporter of
the Church of England. At 70, she was no spring chicken, but her
age had not dimmed her caustic sense of humour, nor diminished
her sharp-eyed insight into character. At a dinner party with the
Bishop of London she had heard of Scott's acceptance for missionary
service in Hawaii, and his detour with the *Tynemouth*. Lady Franklin
had written of her uneasy feelings about him. "I was grieved to
hear that he is a man of unhappy temper and so infatuated with
Popish tendencies ... how he [the Bishop of Honolulu] could think
of taking out such a man."[47]

Lady Franklin was back in England when Scott and the
Tynemouth arrived, but her earlier intuitions about him proved to
be correct. In the Sandwich Islands Scott's grandiose vision for his
mission church soon landed his congregation deeply in debt, and
his evangelical earnestness alienated him from his native
parishioners. Later, he was accused of raping one of his students at
Lahaina and left the islands forever under a cloud of suspicion.[48]

Church service over, the bride-ship women were marched back
to the barracks where they lived under tight security 24 hours a
day. A fence had been erected around the building and its grounds,
and no one except Immigration Committee members were
admitted. A few girls, half-crazy with the endless incarceration,
escaped the first night, but were soon recaptured. It didn't take
long, however, for the single men of the city to figure out the girls'

exercise time in the yard of their compound. Then they gathered regularly at the fences to pass a note, utter a name or whisper an encouraging word to the doleful young women, before the authorities could arrive, shoo the men away and herd the women back inside. Of course, the behaviour of the men at the fences was considered by many to be "disgraceful."[49]

Amor De Cosmos of the *Colonist* took a different view, criticizing the gentry and members of the church for spying. The tone of his copy revealed the depth of his contempt:

> The melancholy discovery [of the meetings at the fence] was made by two clergymen and a naval officer — who for the purpose of making "assurance doubly sure," crawled behind a water-but, with necks outstretched to their utmost length — eyes starting from their sockets with expressions of eager expectancy ... all for the sake of morality.[50]

The court's decision on the *Seaman's Bride* on September 20 became a precedent and it touched the *Tynemouth* story directly as Captain Hellyer was, himself, involved in two lawsuits: one he launched himself against the four most recent mutineers, and one was brought against him by the passengers he had left stranded in San Francisco. Dickson, Campbell and Co., agents for the *Tynemouth*, were quick to see the implications of the *Seaman's Bride* decision, and on September 25, they posted the following notice in the *Colonist*:

> Neither the captain nor the agents will be responsible for any debts contracted by the crew of the Tynemouth.[51]

The disclaimer was well timed.

The crewmen who jumped ship in San Francisco were lucky. A charge of mutiny, justified or not, would not go down well in Admiralty-rich Victoria. At the trial, Captain Hellyer testified before Magistrate Pemberton without any malice toward the accused, as he had done at the trial in the Falklands of those he had detained. Once again, the captain stated that he would readily take back the sailors if they were willing to return to active duty. Hellyer spoke highly of the four stating that "they were all sober and good men and bore good characters."[52] As before, Hellyer had to get the *Tynemouth* home, and he required seasoned, knowledgeable crew.

Magistrate Pemberton was not so accommodating. He warned the prisoners that it was in his power to sentence them to three months' hard labour and the loss of wages. The accused showed little remorse. Alluding to the conditions in the merchant service, one of them stated that "it was better to be uncomfortable for three months than three years, and that they were content to lose the wages."[53] Sensing their disgust at their lack of shipboard rights, Pemberton did not punish them to the full extent of the law. Instead, he gave each of them "one month's hard labor, and ordered the sum of £3, 12s. paid to the captain, as compensation for the trouble he incurred by their refusal to work."[54]

Captain Hellyer's day in court was not a happy one. As fate would have it, he appeared before Pemberton *and* Commander Verney, who had previously pushed for a firm judgment against Wyman. More than that, the disgruntled passengers had hired the best lawyer in the colony, Henry Pering Pellew Crease, who was soon to be attorney-general. It did not augur well for the *Tynemouth* captain.

Mr. Crease opened the case by saying that passengers suffered much discomfort and were compelled to seek financial aid from the British consul, in order to complete their journey to Victoria. Complainant George Hiffe testified that the first mate told him on Thursday, September 11, that the *Tynemouth* would not depart until noon Friday, September 12. When he returned at 8:30 AM the next day, the vessel had left her anchorage and was steaming away, followed by angry passengers in an open longboat. Though Hiffe admitted seeing the "Blue Peter," the international departure flag flying from the yardarm, he didn't see the notice posted near the gangplank on Thursday evening, directing passengers to be back on board by 7:30 AM Friday. Other passengers who, after a night on the town, tried to board the ship in the wee hours of Thursday morning testified they were turned away.

In his defense, Captain Hellyer declared that the first mate had no authority to state a different departure time, especially as the official one had been posted. Hellyer also claimed that the departure flag had been correctly flown and two warning guns fired as required by regulations. On the anchorage in San Francisco Bay, Hellyer claimed the *Tynemouth* was subject to strong adverse tidal currents that Friday morning, and the vessel's early departure was demanded by the San Francisco pilot, who was on board.

On October 17, Magistrates Pemberton and Verney rendered their decision. They did not take kindly to contradictory messages from the master of a merchant vessel and his officers, especially when the welfare of passengers was at stake. Ultimately, they held the captain responsible. Hellyer was found guilty of abandoning passengers in San Francisco, and ordered to pay compensation to them in the amount of £20. Though not as much as Captain Wyman's fine, it was still a significant sum.

In the middle of all this, Amor De Cosmos ran yet another tantalizing headline that perpetuated a rumour that had circulated before the *Tynemouth* arrived:

And More A-Coming

A private letter received in this city by a gentleman from a
relative in London asserts that 500 English women will
arrive in this colony before the middle of December. The
old bachelor hearts will be taken by storm then, and the
unfortunate fellows might as well prepare to capitulate with
good grace. Every Jill among the five hundred is bound to
have her Jack, depend on it.[55]

For De Cosmos, the business was the selling of papers; for him,
the bride-ship sensation had only just begun.

On October 20 the *Tynemouth* steamed out of British Columbia
waters forever. She left with 25 cabin passengers, and 150 in
steerage. The *British Colonist* reported that she also carried $49,000
in gold dust. Immediately upon her return to England in early
1863, Lindsay and Co. put the ship up for sale, and Captain Hellyer
left their service. Eventually, the *Tynemouth* was stranded on the
coast of Denmark on September 17, 1868.

Despite the public criticism, Verney remained full of praise for the
successes the Victoria Female Immigration Committee had achieved
in meeting the challenges posed by the sudden arrival of the *Tynemouth*
women. On the whole, he considered the first bride-ships enterprise
satisfactory, and directed his criticisms to those who had mismanaged
the affair in England. He maintained that the selection procedures for
the women were not strict enough, and felt that most were misled
and misinformed about the conditions and opportunities they would
find in British Columbia when they arrived.

Frederick Whymper wrote bluntly:

Half of them married soon after arrival or went into
service, but a large proportion quickly went to the bad, and,

from appearances, had been there before. The influence of but a few such on the more respectable girls could not have been otherwise than detrimental. To speak gallantly, but truly, many of these ladies were neither young nor beautiful.[56]

By mid-October, when the *Tynemouth* was readying to depart, most journalists had agreed that the bride-ships venture was a limited success. There was one paper, however, that sounded a note of caution. *The Daily Press* wrote:

This is the first shipment. We have no doubt that it will prove to the advantage of the girls, as well as those who may employ them. But as to further shipments we are inclined to the opinion that the Society would do well to exercise much caution, and not be in any haste about sending more until they see their way quite clear. It is doubtless an important work, but it is at the same time, a very delicate and precarious one.[57]

Most of the public, however, had been influenced by the hype surrounding the *Tynemouth* girls' arrival and they paid little notice to those who might dampen their enthusiasm for the next bride-ship, full of single women and already inbound.

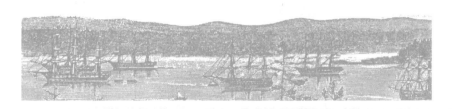

Chapter Seven
THE *ROBERT LOWE*

During the voyage, there were no deaths on board and everyone enjoyed the trip immensely.[1]

Jeremiah Griffiths couldn't believe his eyes. In 114 days flat, the *Robert Lowe* had sailed non-stop, without mishap, halfway round the world. More than that, the ocean-weary, veteran tramp steamer had done it via Cape Horn, where the seas of the great southern oceans were known to swallow ships whole. Just ahead of him was the foremast, and two of its great yardarms were slung round so that they pointed almost directly fore and aft. Though the royals and topgallants were furled, the fore-main and the fore lower-topsail were hauled in tight, so that his view of the crisp, green forests of Vancouver Island was unimpeded. Unlike the formidable wall of white mountains that rose up on the starboard shore, the dark green hills to port were soft and inviting. Even the white-capped blue-green waves of this last, land-locked passage marched in an orderly fashion, toward his new home. It was Saturday, January 10, 1863.

Jeremiah stood mesmerized on the port side for most of that sunny, cold afternoon. He had gone to sea at 16 and knew about ships but the adventure had worn thin. Not only did he find the life hard and dangerous, many of his shipmates had been lost at sea, or simply jumped ship in far-flung ports. Short stints ashore made him realize that England had become a land of misery, so he had diligently saved his money and was now, like millions of others, simply another emigrant. At 23, Jeremiah Griffiths had turned his back on his homeland and put his hopes on British Columbia. Out of the wind, he leaned against the ship's still-warm funnel, and luxuriated in the final moments of being a passenger. Compared to some seas he had experienced, the windy Strait of Juan de Fuca was an absolute joy. The hardest part was over; the rest would be a piece of cake.

Behind him on the mainmast, acres of white canvas were hauled flat so that only the occasional snap of the leech broke the magic of this final afternoon. Farther aft, the second funnel barely smoked, and the mizzenmast with its gaff-rigged spanker was slung out a little to leeward. The vessel creaked and strained as she heeled to the northwesterly which drove her with a will up the strait toward Victoria. The *Robert Lowe* gently rose and fell on the last of the ocean swells, and Jeremiah Griffiths almost felt he didn't want the voyage to finish.

"That old Congalton is a bugger indeed," Jeremiah smiled. "Turn around and you walk smack into extra bloody coal bins lashed on deck. We didn't even see the Falklands." He thought of the *Robert Lowe*'s well-loved captain who had measured out the ship's fuel as if in teaspoons. "Bloody lucky he was, missing storms in the Southern Ocean, bloody lucky." Just as he spoke he heard the order to furl all remaining sail, and felt once more the increased throbbing of the ship's two engines. Great plumes of soot now blew southward, toward the reddening peaks of a ridge in the coastal mountains of Washington Territory. In the Celtic language of his birth, Jeremiah, exuberant that he had made the successful passage in steam, shouted aloud to the belching black smoke that streamed away overhead. "*Infarn cols* [the fires of hell]." He laughed.

The *Robert Lowe,* not missing a beat, made her final, long turn around Race Rocks and steamed toward a very different green and pleasant land.

Griffiths looked at his pocket watch, a gift from his father. "Nearly four o'clock," he mused, "we'll be in just after six." The increasing pulse of the engines triggered a calling forth of the passengers. The decks filled, everyone chatted and Jeremiah thought he heard a cheer. Farther down the deck, crowded together on the rail, he saw Mary Hewitt and Elizabeth Clarke and several other single women that he had met during the long voyage. He hoped he would meet them again in Victoria, and wondered especially if he stood a chance with Mary. The young women jumped and laughed, and could easily have been taken for schoolgirls on an outing. He waved and smiled at them; they waved back and Jeremiah Griffiths thought, at that moment, how good life was.

Owned barely three months by Surrey shipping magnate John Gladstone, the *Robert Lowe* had been sold to William Lindsay of London on January 19, 1855. They appointed a veteran captain, William Congalton, who had skippered her without mishap, first as a troopship through the late 1850s, and then as a tramp steamer, carrying Britain's dispossessed to the colonies. Congalton, like Alfred Hellyer of the *Tynemouth,* was chosen from the ranks of the Royal Navy Reserves. Like Hellyer, he was fair-minded but firm.

Jeremiah Griffiths liked Congalton's quiet style; he had served under some real tyrants. He had left his native Wales and apprenticed as a seaman on the brig *Mary Grace* in 1855, and by 1862, he had accumulated a lifetime of ocean sailing experience. Like most sailors, he was suspicious of the new wedge-shaped clipper ships, such as the *Cainsmore*, that could race from Bombay to Land's End in 60 days — or just as easily disappear without a trace. Confident in the design of the *Robert Lowe* and intrigued by steam, Griffiths favoured the composite ships, the wooden ships with iron frames, the ones with the natural buoyancy of timber that would rise to the seas, time and time again.

Like the other ships in the Lindsay and Co. fleet, the *Robert Lowe* was a single-screw, sail-assisted steamship. Constructed in Cartsdyke, Greenock, Scotland, in 1854, she was wood over iron frames, the great square rivets driven through the planks and clenched tight against the futtocks. This clench-built system made for a very strong hull that was unlikely to open up with the vibration of the engines. She was heavy, 34 feet wide and 240 feet long, and drew 18 feet, with a clipper bow and a rounded stern. Her initial registered tonnage was 1091 tons. The *Robert Lowe* wasn't fast, but she had good lines and was dry and seaworthy. Her namesake, the English parliamentarian and Liberal reformer, Robert Lowe, would have been proud. She could easily be mistaken for the *Tynemouth*, but was just perceptibly smaller. With a main deck and smaller upper deck, her superstructure, especially in the raised poop, clearly revealed her origins in the days of sail. She was a full-rigged ship, with three masts, a long standing bowsprit, and a figurehead of the torso of a proud sailor. Her two in-line steam engines developed a combined thrust of 80 horsepower which, for the day, was considered powerful.

When the *Robert Lowe* dropped anchor in Esquimalt Harbour, the brouhaha caused by the arrival of the *Tynemouth* women, barely three and a half months before, had only just died down. Since that time, one Victoria newspaper, the *Daily Press,* had gone out of business and its rival, the *British Colonist,* chose to prevent another hullabaloo. Its previous foray into sensationalist journalism had fanned the flames of excitement and subjected the *Tynemouth* women to needless scrutiny and humiliation. This time, the manifest of marriageable girls on the *Robert Lowe* would not receive central attention; their coming, in fact, would be played down, and as fate would have it, their arrival was eclipsed by other news.

The *Colonist* editor, Amor De Cosmos, chose to concentrate on the state of the colony's economy:

> The past year has fixed an era in our history. It has cleared away all uncertainties. It has laid the foundation on which the merchant, trader, artisan, practitioner, ship-owner, agriculturist, carrier, capitalist, and real estate owner, may build without fear of extraordinary reaction — on which they may establish themselves for one, five, or ten years and even a lifetime, with the hope of bequeathing fortunes in their lives.[2]

Amidst all this promised bounty, however, there were other, more disturbing signs. The *Colonist* also reported that the ship's company of HMS *Topaze* was busily preparing a benefit concert in the Victoria Theatre for distressed immigrants, while in another section it was noted that an impoverished new arrival had been arrested for stealing a cow.

It was into this curious place that the *Robert Lowe* sailed with its usual paying passengers, and the boatload of sponsored single women.

Arrival of the *Robert Lowe*

This long and anxiously expected vessel has at length arrived in Esquimalt harbor, having cast anchor there on Saturday evening about six o'clock. She left Gravesend on the 18th September last, and has consequently been 114 days en route. She brings 180 passengers of both sexes, among whom are many married ladies come out to join their husbands who are residing here. The weather on the passage was all that could be desired, and not a single spar, we believe, was disturbed or put out of place by the violence of the wind since the ship left England.[3]

All the cheeriness was not entirely accurate, but this first report remained upbeat for most of its length. Captain Congalton and his officers were spoken of "in the highest terms of commendation. The former was kind, courteous, and attentive to the wishes of all on board, and the latter, like true British tars, ably and efficiently gave effect to their commander's wishes."[4] To be sure, Captain Congalton ran a tight ship, but someone had to stoke the furnaces for the steam boilers for 114 continuous days. In the light of the two mutinies on board the *Tynemouth*, still fresh in the reporters' minds, no one, it seems, bothered or was directed to interview members of the crew. The happy tone continued with the reporting of an event en route:

Three interesting little cherubs were added to the community on board during the voyage, and we are happy

to state that under the judicious care and kind treatment
of the surgeon of the ship, Dr. Ash, both mothers and
infants are, in common with the rest of the passengers, in
excellent health.[5]

All that was printed of the passage outward bound was that the
vessel, "did not touch at any port coming out."[6] Captain Congalton
was highly praised for provisioning his vessel with ample pure water,
food and coal. The usual stop at the Falkland Islands had been
deemed unnecessary.

There were only two brief hints that there was more to the voyage
of the *Robert Lowe* than was revealed to the public at large. The
first concerned the ship's stores, and recalled the recent case against
the *Seaman's Bride*:

We understand however, that had the time of arrival been
protracted a week longer, the store of edibles would have
been well nigh exhausted.[7]

The second intimation was a single line of copy that simply stated,
"We regret to say that six of the hands deserted the vessel on
Saturday night."[8] Beyond that cryptic statement, nothing.

Readers salivating for information on the bride-ship women first
had to read De Cosmos's view that the 14 gentlemen, 5 merchants
and a chemist on board were "gentlemen of capital and enterprise,"
and were intended to engage in "mercantile pursuits, for which
they have a good field to work upon here."[9]

When news of the young women on board was finally given, it
was sparse and unsatisfying. Among the passengers, the *British
Colonist* admitted, were 36 women from Manchester, "sent out
by the philanthropic Miss Rye."[10] The girls were deemed

exemplary in character to have been afforded assistance, and their dutiful chaperones, Reverend W. S. Reece and his wife, were completely above reproach. Of their accommodations, little was said except:

> On board ship they occupied a separate compartment, never being allowed to mingle with the other passengers, and for the fatherly solicitude and scrupulous care bestowed upon them by the Captain, that gentleman has entitled himself to the lasting gratitude of the girls and the community.[11]

Maria Rye had left the Female Middle-Class Emigration Society only months before, because she felt the organization had become blinded by its feminist organizers who wished to increase the emigration of independent gentlewomen, albeit without means, as a statement of its feminist ideology. Maria believed that jobs, not ideology, were the first requisite for women, and felt that lower-class working girls had a better chance of finding employment, and its attendant freedom, in the colonies. She chose to set out on her own and help girls thrown out of work by the closure of the cotton mills in Lancashire.

Perhaps part of the reason for the *British Colonist*'s muted stance in covering the arrival of the *Robert Lowe* was an error of its own making. Three months before, the *British Colonist* reported that the next bride-ship, due to arrive in the middle of December, would contain 500 single and eager young women. What arrived on the *Robert Lowe* were three dozen uneducated working girls between the ages of 12 and 19 from the midlands, whose livelihood had suddenly disappeared. The *British Colonist* editor distanced himself from the marriageable aspect of the bride-ship project; there would be no reported "Jill for every Jack" and the tone of the coverage would instead be patronizing and one of moral obligation:

> They will be welcomed by many families in this city who have been in need for some time of respectable female servants; and we trust the poor friendless creatures will be placed in no other kind of establishments.[12]

The *Colonist* stated that the previous fiasco caused by the women's committee's failure to prepare the Marine Barracks for the *Tynemouth* girls would not be repeated for those on the *Robert Lowe*. De Cosmos was pleased to report that the barracks were scrubbed and readied by men especially hired and supervised. "Nothing but provisions remains to be ordered."[13] If the women's arm of the Victoria Female Immigration Committee was involved, they received no press at all.

The report did its best to prevent the carnival-like atmosphere it had helped create with the arrival of the first bride-ship:

> There is not the slightest necessity for any parade about so simple a matter as the landing of a few passengers, and we cannot conceive anything more heartless or ill-considered than to have poor young strangers, we don't care of what sex, subjected to the rude gaze of a motley crowd of roughs, who, instead of running about idle, should be engaged with the shovel or the axe earning an honest living. We know right well the committee are composed of men of the most benevolent dispositions, and actuated by the purest and best of motives, but they must not allow their zeal to run counter to the dictates of common sense and prudence, in carrying out their arrangements.[14]

If the state of the colony's economy was one major newsworthy item that allowed De Cosmos to shift his attention away from the *Robert Lowe*'s cargo, the other issue, paradoxically, was the one that brought the young women to Vancouver Island and British Columbia in the first place. Barely a week after the arrival of the *Robert Lowe*, a *British Colonist* subscriber sent a letter and £50 to initiate a fund for the thousands of people suffering sudden unemployment in the cotton-manufacturing districts of England.

The calamity unfolding in the midlands was very real, and the *British Colonist* rose to it with all the high-blown rhetoric aimed previously at the bride-ship enterprise:

> Lancashire Distress
> When we read of the thousands and tens of thousands of able-bodied Englishmen with wives and children in a state of absolute want and wretchedness, it is enough to stir up the coldest heart, and draw a tear of pity from the most stoical among us ... Hunger is their daily visitant: famine the dread intruder that has entered unbidden and taken up his place at one side of the family hearth, and no doubt ere long disease and death will occupy the other.[15]

Clearly, the idea of the stricken family had struck an emotional chord with the paper's editor, and De Cosmos used it to support the subscriber's call for contributions:

> The strong man will soon be reduced to weakness, and in that emaciated condition must look to those near and dear to him — his wife and children — pining and wasting away before his eyes, without the power or ability to administer

relief or sustenance to them. It is harrowing to think of able-bodied man growing weaker and weaker — of delicate females daily growing more faint and less able to bear the destitution that is upon them.[16]

The rhetoric worked because the Lancashire Relief Fund sponsored by the *Colonist* soon elicited £98 from various members of the Victoria gentry.[17] The girls from Manchester on the *Robert Lowe,* in the light of the reported conditions in the midlands, had become refugees, more than brides. Eagerly sought after as domestics in the colony, they were a way in which genteel families in Victoria could help an ailing motherland. In response to the Lancashire distress, De Cosmos also modified his own views about the financial well-being of the colony. He did admit to some poverty in Victoria at the time, but believed that the "temporary difficulties" would "soon entirely disappear from our midst."[18]

The wages the Immigration Committee had set for the young domestics from the *Tynemouth* or the *Robert Lowe* would not make anyone rich. At £25 per year, they were comparable to wages paid to women in domestic service in Britain, but Britain's economy was failing, and a surplus of female servants had kept wages low. In British Columbia, two recent gold rushes had created an economy that was still booming, and for well-off families, domestic servants were in very short supply. Moreover, those young women who entered service *without* the help of the Immigration Committee often made more than double its recommended salary. One such independent domestic wrote home:

> I have got a situation and a very happy one. Mrs. —— is such a gentle, kind lady, and three such good, well behaved children. I have $74 a year wages.[19]

Victoria families who hired the bride-ship women knew they were getting a very good deal, and while they could, they kept quiet about it. Yet, even at these independent salaries, a young domestic had to leave home forever, work in a household far more hours than in a cotton mill and be subject again to the old distinctions of rank and class.

The situation for those single women who had emigrated as governesses was even worse. Very few positions were available for them, and in consequence, their wages were low. Educated though they were, they were also too genteel to organize for more money; to do so would have meant adopting tactics considered below their station. Only a few governesses had the flexibility to react to the real conditions on the frontier, and these survived by abandoning their education and their class and taking up something else.

The teenage orphans on the *Robert Lowe* couldn't know any of this; they were pleased to accept whatever wage was given. Once the girls figured out the real nature of the gold-driven economy, it was no wonder that, in British Columbia as in England, many domestics married as soon as possible. Others, seeing even greater opportunity, quit their households altogether to become businesswomen in their own right, and gain a share of the riches the two colonies had to offer.

Sunday, January 11, was a day of rest and quarantine on board the *Robert Lowe*. Probably the Reverend Reece held a service for all the ship's company. Beyond that there was little activity. It was cold on the anchorage in Esquimalt basin, and passengers must have been bored and anxious with the icy morning decks that they had walked around a thousand times before.

On Monday morning, January 12, the action began in earnest. By noon, the steamer *Emily Harris* had come alongside and taken aboard 150 of the passengers for the brief jaunt into Victoria's inner harbour. The single women who had travelled under the auspices of Maria Rye were left behind. The paying passengers disembarked first and it was they who attracted immediate attention. Whether the men gathering ashore thought that the single girls were aboard the *Emily Harris* is unknown, but the sight of the little vessel steaming slowly down the harbour created excitement that no amount of prudent journalism could quell.

As the rumours flew, the pubs emptied and soon a vast crowd of well-liquored bachelors had established itself on Union Wharf. News or no news, they were not now about to be thwarted by anyone. When Captain Pike turned his vessel slightly toward Rock Bay Bridge, the throng suddenly got the notion that the *Emily Harris* would land at the new Janion, Green, & Rhodes Wharf farther on. So, like a group of Keystone Cops after the robbers, off they raced in hot pursuit. Suddenly the *Emily Harris* turned again, this time heading back toward Brodrick's Wharf where she finally landed. Again the rabble wheeled, now more frenzied than ever.

By the time the *Emily Harris* had made fast, the pushing and shoving crowd had turned ugly. As the men raced about this way and that, accusations arose as to who had caused the frequent changes of direction, because the actions had cost many in the mob the best locale from which to ogle the women. Threats, shouts and waving fists filled the air. Suddenly all movement ceased, and two men squared off to face each other. Silence. Then, almost directly in front of the *Emily Harris,* a wild fistfight began between the two. The crowd gathered to cheer and jeer accordingly. Clothes were torn, blood was spilt and profanity split the air and for ten minutes, the welcoming throng forgot the newcomers from the *Robert Lowe*. Thoughts of brides and love had been momentarily displaced by the call for blood.

As quickly as it began, it was over. As arms were dusted off, and collars and coats re-aligned, people suddenly remembered where they were. Chagrined, they moved slowly, caps in hand, toward the *Emily Harris* at the end of the wharf. The newly arrived wives and their husbands had, during the brawl, quietly taken themselves away, and the few male passengers left on board moved quickly through the crowd and disappeared. The *British Colonist* could not resist reporting the incident with its usual feisty irony:

> The utmost disorder prevailed, and the newcomers must have been highly impressed with a deep sense of the efficient police regulations of the colony.[20]

The single women were nowhere to be seen. Then, amid all the gossip, someone remembered out loud that the *Tynemouth* girls had been landed in front of the Legislative Buildings on James Bay, and that this might be done again. When that idea took hold, along with the realization that single women were still imminent, the rush to the waterfront became a stampede. The *British Colonist* followed the story, corrected the numbers, and offered with moderation:

> At about half past 3 o' clock, the Grappler steamed into the harbor, having on board 38 single females with several other passengers, and Captain Congalton.[21]

Commander Verney was, as before, on hand in HMS *Grappler* and quick to offer the girls the short trip ashore. Verney certainly noticed the girls, but found them this time less beguiling and less attractive than those he had met on the *Tynemouth*. He echoed the sentiments first noted by De Cosmos:

This afternoon I took them all round to Victoria in the ship, and landed them there: they are evidently of a lower class than those who came in the Tynemouth; and perhaps better suited for the colony on the whole. [22]

As the HMS *Grappler* steamed up the inner harbour, Captain Moore on the steamer *Flying Dutchman,* anchored in West Bay, dipped the ensign — proper etiquette for the Royal Navy — and then her burgee, in honour of the girls' safe arrival. Moore's crew, seeing the young women pass speedily by, gave three resounding cheers. The *Dutchman's* gesture was almost the last civilized act of authorized protocol that would greet the girls that afternoon.

HMS *Grappler* rounded up and let go her anchor. The girls, however, did not immediately gather on the deck. Instead, only two were seen and they were heavily clothed, supported by naval officers, and placed gently in a Royal Navy tender that headed off in the direction of West Bay. It was tuberculosis. As fast and efficient as the *Robert Lowe* was, she couldn't outrun the pervasive damp of a long sea voyage. The disease had flared up again in the two girls and they were now gravely ill; try as they might, the staff at the naval squadron hospital could not save them and a few days later, they died.

In the excitement of the moment, no one seemed to question if any of the other girls had been infected by the unfortunate two. No general long-term quarantine was declared and the sight of the sick young women seemed little more than a diversion from the main event. The gawking crowd that had momentarily hushed suddenly regained its voice. Cheers broke out as two of *Grappler's* boats were lowered and filled finally with the promised prize. Each boat made two short trips to the good earth, something the girls had not stepped on for over three and a half months.

The greeting at the waterfront was heartfelt, if formal, as members of the Immigration Committee welcomed the young women, and shook hands with Captain Congalton and Reverend Reece and his wife. Reverend Edward Cridge of Christ Church Cathedral was there to greet them, as were Mrs. Harris, the mayor's wife, and several other notable ladies of the community. Dr. Davie, who was also present, apparently did not notice any more overly reddened faces, a sure sign of "galloping tuberculosis."

Since September, when the *Tynemouth* had arrived, the walk up from the waterfront on James Bay to the Marine Barracks had deteriorated considerably. The winter rains had turned the once expansive green and open ground into a sodden quagmire, and the Immigration Committee had laid a narrow wooden boardwalk to protect themselves and the new arrivals from floundering in the mud. The boardwalk idea backfired. Planned as protection, it became an alleyway along which the young women were compelled to walk. The mob, which had grown steadily to over a thousand, swarmed along both sides of the planks like cattle at a feeding trough.

The fun for the crowd started when each woman began to move along the narrow boardwalk, eyeballed closely by each and every hopeful bachelor. For the young girls from the *Robert Lowe*, the humour was lost in humiliation. The girls had to run the gauntlet amid the utterance of jokes.[23]

Perhaps the fight at Brodrick's Wharf had tired the men. Perhaps it was the gentle remonstrances of Dr. Davie and the Reverend Cridge. Perhaps it was the very nearness of the women themselves. Whatever the reason, the comments of the men as the girls walked by never degenerated into anything more than the "oohs and aahs" of projected desire. No man stepped out of the crowd with a miner's poke and an offer of marriage, though the young females from the Manchester mills elicited such smiles as they had probably not seen since, in another time, they had given their pay packets to mother and father at home. Even De Cosmos was surprised enough to admit, "We must say that the majority of those present were well conducted."[24] What didn't surprise him, however, was the action of the city's administration, and its usual ineffective contribution to the civil peace:

> Four policemen were upon the spot, out of uniform, and without an officer, who might just as well have been absent, for they evidently had no instructions.[25]

George Hills, Bishop of British Columbia, went to see the new arrivals in the Marine Barracks the day after they landed. He had offered Reverend Reece and his wife the use of his own residence until they were settled and of the girls he wrote:

> They are cheerful and contented. They are principally Factory workers from Lancashire. Plain simple young women. I was pleased to see their heartiness and zeal in coming forward to greet Mr. Reece as we approached, a true Lancashire fashion.[26]

They may have been open with Reverend Reece, but they weren't all as honourable as Hills wanted to believe. Maria Rye was not running a philanthropic organization; in fact, just the opposite was true. Her society had teetered on the edge of bankruptcy since its inception, and sponsorship on the *Robert Lowe* meant that the girls' fare to Victoria would be loaned to them with the legal obligation that it would be paid back as soon as they were placed in service in Victoria. Eighteen months after their arrival, five of the girls, Jane Atkinson, Charlotte Bates, Ann Fish, Jane Smith and Bessie Lyons, were charged with neglecting to pay the amount still outstanding on their fares. The lack of honour, or memory, was nowhere more evident than in the case of Charlotte Bates, who had, in the meantime, married.[27]

Maria Rye's instincts in putting jobs before politics had proven correct, and by the end of January 1863, 20 of the orphan girls had already been placed in domestic service in homes around the city. For the educated gentlewomen, it was a different story. As predicted, several governesses from the *Tynemouth* still remained out of work and were living in the barracks some four months after their arrival. What remained now for all of them, employed or not, was to accept the limitations of their occupations and either embrace marriage, children and a richer domesticity or strike out on their own and be empowered by the experience. Some of them moved as far from the sea as they could possibly get.

Seven years at sea on the *Mary Grace* was enough for Jeremiah Griffiths, or so he thought when he arrived in Victoria on the *Robert Lowe*. He found work almost immediately on the docks as a longshoreman with the Hudson's Bay Company. Nineteen years later, Jeremiah was still there; at 43, in 1882, he had become the company's head wharfinger. Along the way, he refitted an old schooner, the *Jenny Jones*, and made two short trips with her up the Gulf of Georgia to settlements along its inland fiords. When she was converted into a coastal steamer in her last days, Jeremiah returned to shore life. He soon became chief wharfinger for the Canadian Pacific Navigation Company, and remained there till the end.

Chapter Eight
THE WIFE EXPERIMENT RECONSIDERED

Maiden, dear maiden, thou hast come far to me,
A frail bark has borne thee across the dark sea;
As a vision of hope, swift gladness you bring —
Swift as the sky-birds to the clouds where they spring.
As the rose to the desert, the flower to the bee,
Maiden, dear maiden, so thou art to me.[1]

The attempt at social engineering that brought the bride-ships to British Columbia died almost completely with the departure of the *Robert Lowe*. Interest in Victoria was already dwindling when on July 14, 1863, the Reverend Edward Cridge, rector of Christ Church Cathedral and chair of the Victoria Immigration Committee, sent Governor James Douglas a bill for services rendered. Those services were for alterations and repairs made to the Marine Barracks in connection with the *Tynemouth*'s arrival, but Cridge was quick to add that a bill for the care of the girls from the *Robert Lowe* would also be forthcoming. Douglas paid the bill, but Cridge's advice that "your Excellency's Government should take such steps as may seem proper to procure the shipment of more females of the working class to this colony,"[2] fell on deaf ears. The wife experiment in British Columbia, for the moment at least, was dead in the water. The two founding agencies, the Columbia Emigration Society and the feminist Female Middle-Class Emigration Society, never again sponsored poor, single women domestics or governesses. However, there were a few final flutters.

The Congregationalist minister, Reverend Matthew Macfie, had been in the public eye before. In 1861, he had lambasted the Anglican Church in the press for its refusal to sanctify white/ aboriginal marriages, and in 1863 had been one of many who criticized the bride-ships organizers for allowing a few "bad eggs" to place the morality of the young women in some jeopardy. Just over a year after the *Robert Lowe* left, he was at it again, this time responding to the Legislative Assembly's decision to promote female immigration with direct funding. In March 1864, Macfie called a mass meeting in Victoria's Lyceum Hall. He had received Mayor Harris's endorsement as immigration lecturer in England, and was trying to muster public support as the person who would disseminate "proper and reliable information" about Vancouver Island and the mainland colony to those interested in leaving the mother country. Macfie thought the issue of female immigration would garner him further approval:

He was sure that 500 respectable girls brought out in small detachments would be immediately absorbed. He would not lead these girls to believe that husbands were waiting for them on the wharves, and that proposals of marriage would be made to each of them in a few hours, but that they might all get respectable places at a high rate of wages.[3]

Macfie argued that he knew of many well-to-do gentlemen in Victoria who "were obliged to go to California to secure partners for life because they could not find them here."[4] However, many in the packed assembly saw through Macfie's maneuverings, given the hefty $3,000 stipend which accompanied the "ambassadorship," not to mention the opportunity the role would offer in luring converts to his particular brand of religious revivalism. Macfie never did gain public support and soon afterward, the mainland colony backed out of a similar government-supported scheme, fearing the affair would lead to a repetition of the chaos of the arrival of the *Robert Lowe*. Once again, the bride-ships enterprise seemed certain to be scuttled.

Where legitimate plans failed to encourage females to the colony, a nefarious scheme attempted to fill the void. In July 1865, one enterprising San Francisco businessman shipped the first contingent of eight prostitutes to Victoria in what promised to be a lucrative, on-going affair. Bishop Hills believed it was "crime enough to call down judgement from God."[5] Ironically, the paddle-wheel steamer *Brother Jonathan,* on which they sailed, was lost off the California coast and most of the passengers drowned.

By 1868, interest was again revived when it was learned that Maria Rye would arrive in Canada in May with the "first batch of 100 women" bound for Ontario. With local domestic servants able to demand upwards of $20 a month, and decent, well-to-do farmers unable to get wives at any price, the *British Columbian* urged that Governor Seymour "would do well to place himself in correspondence with Miss Rye."[6] In March 1869, Seymour, by then a chronic alcoholic, readily agreed to the assembly's proposal to appoint a local board of immigration to oversee and promote female immigration.

The Female Immigration Board suggested that a family who wished a servant should pay an organizational fee for the screening and arranging passage of an English domestic and settled finally on the sum of $150. Of that amount, the government would pay $50, while the remainder would be paid by the family in two instalments — $50 on a servant's departure from Britain, and $50 upon her arrival in Victoria. The domestic would then be bound to the sponsoring family for two years during which time she would make arrangements to repay the money spent on her behalf. Initially it was believed that a government grant of $5,000 would permit 40 young women per year to emigrate to British Columbia, but criticism forced the assembly to reduce the grant and lower the number of sponsored girls to 20. More, those families who participated in the endeavour were allowed to submit promissory notes to the board in lieu of cash.

Not everyone was pleased with the new arrangements. Dr. John Helmcken argued that government funding should not support exclusively female emigration, but should focus instead upon families and their immediate relations. "Why not bring out the wives and children of those already here, and who intend to settle? The female relatives of these people would come with them, and they would be servants at first, afterwards [they] would make wives for our settlers."[7] Others wanted assisted immigration for agricultural labourers, as well as for servant girls, and still others wanted the whole scheme to be free. Clearly the government needed help.

By chance, Bishop Hills and his wife were planning a trip to England in the spring of 1869, and it was decided that he should be given $400 to follow up on requests from members of the Victoria bourgeoisie who, desirous of servants, had already contacted friends in the old country. Beyond those arrangements, Hills was also to find new domestic servants wishing to emigrate. At the same time, it was understood that "His Lordship, while in England, would seek co-operation with the British Board of Immigration,"[8] and not "fail to visit Downing Street"[9] looking to gain further financial support for the revived colonial venture.

However, Governor Seymour, now drunk most of the time, had forgotten to advise the Colonial Office of British Columbia's re-involvement in a bride-ships project. By the time Hills began his rounds in Britain, Governor Seymour was dead of acute alcohol poisoning, and many high-ranking English civil servants greeted Hills's entreaties with stone-faced ignorance.

Government assistance for female immigration under the local board turned out to be $2,000 per year, with advances of $100 paid to the head of each family who wished a servant. Though the Christian origins of the bride-ships enterprise had shifted to a civil authority, the matrimonial intent of the whole operation was never more clear:

> Let them be plainly told that if our families want servants, our settlers want wives; and that the manner in which they may fulfill their agreements as servants shall be the best test of their fitness to enter women's highest and holiest sphere of action. With a given number of girls arriving early, families could afford to part with those already in service to make glad the hearts of settlers, and thus secure for the colony a permanent and thrifty population.[10]

There was much interest in Bishop Hills's proceedings on behalf of the Female Immigration Board, and several notable Victoria citizens, in London at the time, sent regular dispatches to the colony's papers to keep citizens informed. One such chronicler was Victoria businessman Alfred Waddington, who was in the English capital to raise interest in his plan for a northern road through the coast mountains to Bute Inlet and his even more far-fetched dream of a trans-continental railway across Canada to British Columbia. Waddington reported that Hills was busy "forwarding the schemes of Female Immigration with characteristic energy." Hills had been in communication not only with Whitehall, but also with the mandarins of the Hudson's Bay Company. It was Waddington's opinion that British Columbia's subsidized emigration policy had been favourably received and that the first shipment of female domestics was a fait accompli, and would "probably be by the H.B.C. barque, *Prince of Wales*."[11]

However, other more powerful voices in Britain were at work condemning the idea of government support for any schemes of subsidized emigration. Lord Granville believed in "well-conducted" emigration, but feared "that any project for carrying it on by means of loans to the intended emigrants will disappoint the expectations of those who set it afoot."[12] Granville held out little hope that such requests would ever make it through the British parliament.

Pressing on regardless, agents of Victoria's Female Immigration Board in England had, by the autumn of 1869, found enough unemployed single young women for their venture to enable them to secure letters of contract, a matron and a vessel. It wasn't to be the Hudson's Bay Company's *Prince of Wales*, but a less expensive, older, full-rigged freighter out of Oslo. She would depart from Liverpool.

On January 10, 1870, the barque *Alpha*, under Captain N. A. Nielson, left the River Mersey bound for Victoria, with the last group of young women ever to be a part of the bride-ships project. What space was left from her thousand tons of freight had been consigned to an English matron and 21 other female passengers, who had been engaged as domestic servants to well-off families in British Columbia. Since there were no other passengers on board, the women were not restricted to a particular part of the ship. Like Congalton of the *Robert Lowe* and Porter of the *Marcella*, Captain Nielson received unanimous praise from the girls and he spoke highly of his charming and animated guests. "The conduct of these girls during the entire passage was in perfect accord with the written characters [the board] received in England." Unlike previous bride-ships, the *Alpha* suffered no storms or illness en route, and despite the five-month-long voyage, the "immigrants were all clearly healthy and well behaved."[13]

There were, however, a few skeptics in Victoria who spread rumours doubting the *Alpha*'s suitability for carrying passengers on a voyage half way around the world. Perhaps the horror stories from the *Tynemouth* had over-stimulated the rumourmongers' imaginations; the gentlemen of the Female Immigration Board, quick to allay such criticism, initiated a thorough investigation of the ship immediately upon her arrival in Esquimalt, and she was declared clean, seaworthy and well provisioned.

No fuss was made of the girls' disembarkation, the only spectacle being the delight the young women expressed when they were finally brought ashore and the touching sight of their parting, after their months together at sea. Tears and hugs over, the girls were whisked away immediately to their respective homes throughout the city. The Female Immigration Board was "most gratified" that all parties, on both sides of the Atlantic, had carried off their particular tasks with organization and dispatch.

If the press lauded the civil authority for this last bride-ships venture, they also took the opportunity to advise the upper-class families who had sponsored a servant of their responsibility toward the colony's new citizens:

Need we ask those in this community to whose charge these girls have been confided to think of their lonely and trying position, and, as far as circumstances may permit, act a maternal part towards them? Do not quite lose sight of the sister in the servant.

Remember that they are human beings, in many respects with like passions and aspirations, and think that the very loneliness and utter dependence of their situation only augments the responsibility of those to whose charge they have been committed.[14]

Humane and patronizing feelings aside, the government-supported female immigration policy was not widely accepted. "Let us have assisted immigration of all classes," wrote one disgruntled family man. "There is but one way: By petitioning the Home Government to remove the purple-and-fine-linen staff of officials and provide us with a simpler form of government with working men at its head."[15] The more accountable form of government that would deal with immigration on a wider scale was, in the minds of many, no longer in Britain but in confederation with Canada. Six months before British Columbia entered Confederation, and six months after the *Alpha* dropped anchor in Esquimalt, an official of the province's legislature wrote the Colonial Office in London, suspending further joint female immigration activity. The bride-ships endeavour was finished.

Certain patterns emerge that suggest that the enterprise, with its lofty goals, was doomed from the outset. Three views become clear. First, the London women's movement, which believed in placing single educated gentlewomen in the colonies to uphold and advance the cause of feminism on the frontier, found itself facing an uncomfortable paradox of class: the independent upper-class governess was fast becoming the handmaiden of the rising middle class. Second, the ideal of a Christian society in British Columbia, hermetically sealed against temptation and inter-racial union by Church of England dogma, was unrealistic. This vision, of a compliant and faithful Christian family on the frontier, fostered by Anglican missionaries such as Lundin Brown and supported by the Columbia Mission Society, ignored the urges of human sexuality. Third, the conditions that shaped the kind of society the women actually found, once they arrived, were far more powerful than either of the two contrasting ideologies of women's liberation and Anglican acquiescence. The social code of this new and empty land far outweighed any obligations of the so-called new "role" of women or the call of faith. In a landscape as immense as British Columbia, in which protocol, class, religion and history had little sway, Christian and feminist ideologues did not get their way with the bride-ship women.

The excess of single Englishwomen in general, and an oversupply of genteel, educated, single women in particular, should have been an easy problem to solve. All that was required was an organizing body to oversee the emigration of these women. However, that wasn't easy because the idea of a colonial matrimonial marketplace for single women was in complete opposition to the aim of female independence, free from the constraints of the prevailing marital patriarchy.

The more the London Female Middle-Class Emigration Society tried to find work for educated gentlewomen, the more some members were perplexed by the inherent contradiction: the position of the colonial governess actually lowered the status and power of the women that early feminists sought to help. A governess was required to be subservient to the growing middle class that hired her, yet she usually came from the upper class, and this was something that high-class feminists simply could not endure.

It was the woman of a middle-class household who was freed from labour by employing a governess, and a governess did not raise the lower classes — they simply passed her by on their way up, while she was reduced to a symbol of middle-class wealth. She was not an agent of social liberation; she was simply stuck in an often-thankless rut. More, the very term "governess" had little political power. Pay was notoriously low and joining what little union activity there was, was often seen as a betrayal of the class from which they had come. In an age when even the women in the cotton factories finally became militant, the governess was still considered a "lady," a product of the leisure class who simply did not make a fuss. The governess "was at best envied and at worst the object of mild scorn, and all she sought was survival in genteel obscurity."[16] So, if employment demeaned her class and bettered another, and marriage was thought to be untenable, the Victorian governess with an inclination toward feminism was caught in a trap of her own making. She was damned if she married, and damned if she did not — the classic paradox.

When Maria Rye founded her Female Middle-Class Emigration Society, she had some fairly grandiose notions about the worth of educated women in the colonies. She believed that the "vice and immorality"[17] of colonial life would be diminished simply by the presence of a higher class of women. This lofty outlook was shattered when she discovered that British Columbia didn't want governesses at all.

On July 26, 1862, only a month after the *Tynemouth* set sail, Colonel Richard Moody, Commander of the Royal Engineers in New Westminster, published a letter in the *Times* of London. He sounded one of many death-knells to Maria Rye's dreams:

I am sorry to say that the opening for educated women here is at present very slender. Household work is what is demanded. Our wives, the ladies of the colony from the highest to the humblest, have to labor in the kitchen, the nursery, and the washhouse ... Washerwomen are the nuggets in our domestic economy. You would be justified in including any number to emigrate, and good nurses for young children also. "Maids of all work" would be received with open arms.[18]

No doubt Moody was writing from the perspective of his overworked wife, Mary, who had seven children, five of them under the age of six. Mary definitely needed domestic, not high-class, help.

Moody was by no means alone in his view. The Reverend Alexander Pringle also spoke out against those who would send governesses to the edge of the wilderness where there were few families and no children:

I hear that Rev. Garrett has been advocating BC as a fine field for the settlement of decayed gentlewomen — Oh dear! Who could have filled his Irish imagination with such ideas — for mercies sake, do all you can to stop such insanity! The market in Victoria is already stocked with ladies, employing themselves in needlework, keeping millinery shops — in fact grievously disappointed at the number of people who do *not* want governesses and ladies to do the work which we want to get out of a pair of hard hands and brawny arms.[19]

The feminists, if they were really interested in female liberation, needed to become a little less bound by their own ideology and give women a more tangible measure of independence — money, in the guise of work. The emigrant women themselves led the way. Annie Davis, a governess who went to Australia, wrote:

> Were I in the position of a third or fourth rate Governess in England, I would unhesitatingly become a domestic servant in Australia ... I have no doubt it would require some common sense and humility for such a Governess to become a servant, and she would find herself infinitely better off. If my words could reach some of my toiling sisters at home I would say "Be sensible, undergo a little domestic training and come out here ... "[20]

Maria Rye saw the light; she left the movement she had founded and turned her attention to the emigration of working-class women in the Manchester cotton co-operatives. By the late 1860s, she was in contact with the government of Canada, looking to organize emigration of girls to Ontario; she had already helped 350 women from the midlands emigrate to New Zealand, where her ideas about women and work were well received.

The Anglican missionaries needed the women the way they needed the Indian — to justify their work on the frontier. Boatloads of good Christian women were necessary to help reclaim the rowdy white males and restore the purity of the Christian family. The educated English governess, who might sell out feminist aims or fail to plunge into the hard life on the edge of the wilderness, was rejected by all: the church, the feminists and the colonial family.

At the outset of the bride-ships story, the men in the Anglican Church co-opted boatloads of young women for their own ends; the feminists, too, needed the women, or a distinct class of them, to counter the influence of unschooled white males who represented patriarchal dominance in the colonies. All these organizers of the bride-ships professed to aim for social change but what they really wanted was social control. As the women they brought spread out across the landscape of the frontier, the control they had sought was never achieved.

Chapter Nine
DIFFUSION: ICE CRYSTALS ON GLASS

And not by eastern windows only,
When daylight comes, comes in the light;
In front the sun climbs slow, how slowly!
But westward, look, the land is bright![1]

And what did the women of the bride-ships want for
themselves? In the absence of women's diaries, such as
the one kept by Mary MacLean who emigrated to
Australia, only their actions remain as their voice. It is clear that of
the women whose stories are known, all wanted marriage, and all
achieved it, to varying degrees.

Emma Lazenby had seen alcoholic despair in the Yorkshire dales
of her youth and wished only to alleviate it here. On the frontier,
Florence Wilson could have a drink and love whomever she wished.
Jane Saunders, who once kneaded bread as a scullery maid, ended
up managing others who did the same in a fine Victoria household.
Emily Ann Morris who, as a girl, cleaned barns, lived to own a
livery stable. Martha Clay, Augusta Jane Morris and Sophia Shaw

were all able to pass land on to their children. Emma Tammadge, Louisa Townsend and Mary Macdonald gained entry into Victoria's gentry, a distinction and class earned largely through their gifted husbands. Margaret Faussett became a teacher and Maria Duren remained sweetly anonymous with her beloved shipboard doctor.

FLORENCE WILSON

It didn't take long after she stepped off the *Tynemouth* for Florence Wilson to figure out that the life of a governess in Victoria wasn't what she wanted. She knew she was too impatient to be good with young children, especially spoiled ones, and she hated the rigidity of a social system that told her even where to sit. Florence didn't want to *be* somebody. Papa had been somebody, and he wasn't happy. Florence ached to actually *do* something, though for the longest time she wasn't sure what it would be. The first step had been the hardest; now there was no looking back.

For the first few months Florence was in Victoria, she made clothes for the well-heeled Helmcken family. By January of 1863, she had opened a small stationery and fancy goods shop on Government Street, adjoining the St. Nicholas Hotel. It flourished and for a year it gave her the freedom to develop an interest in acting that had been stifled in childhood. Her new life began with selling tickets to the Fireman's Ball at the Lyceum Theatre and it ended with her a theatrical legend in the Cariboo.

With the same impulses that drove the miners to the goldfields, Florence went north on Barnard's first express to Barkerville. Like the Reverend John Sheepshanks and the other educated itinerants on the frontier, she took her books — all 130 of them. By June 1864, she had become the first and only librarian in Camerontown *and* in British Columbia.

In the early 1860s Barkerville had become the centre of the Cariboo Gold Rush, its population in excess of 5,000. Florence knew that the free-and-easy nights of music in the bars, punctuated with occasional touring so-called "professional" performers such as Tom Lafont, the Champion Whistler of the World, were not enough. Separated from home and women and facing daily hardship, the miners needed sentiment, but they needed it with the safety valve of farce. In 1865, the Cariboo Amateur Dramatic Association was formed, and Florence and her friend, Emily Edwards, soon became renowned and respected members.

By 1868, the Parlor Saloon was purchased by the dramatic society, and with a modest conversion it became the first "Theatre Royale." Florence and Emily spent long nights making multiple longhand copies of popular one-act farces from the only Samuel French anthology in town. Topical burlesques such as *The Mad Hatter* and *D'ye Know Me Now* played to packed houses. When they became proficient, Florence and the others wrote their own productions.

On September 16, 1868, the Theatre Royale, along with the rest of Barkerville, burned to the ground. Of course it rose again, Phoenix-like, within six months, and so did its beloved theatre. This time, however, the Theatre Royale opened above the new firehall, which sported an alarm bell in the belfry.

As the miners' friend Florence was their equal. To many around the town, she was simply "Florence." As an actress, she became known widely as "Miss Florence." In this guise, she could play the heroine, the sister, the lover and occasionally the matron, as the script defined. Florence had escaped the dictates of the Church of England, and had redefined herself on her own terms among people she had grown to love.

In May 1869, Florence and some friends took out eight hill claims on Williams Creek, and formed the "Florence Co." mining venture.[2] She did so because six months before, she had taken the real plunge and opened her own saloon, the Phoenix.

Now as a publican in her own saloon, Florence Wilson could play her finest role; she could play a guardian angel, den mother and confidante to her heart's content, and she would nurse the sick and mend the wounded.

In 1873, Florence moved her business to the settlement of Stanley on Lightning Creek. She operated a saloon-cum-roadhouse, and stayed for the two years of the boom. By 1875 she was back in Barkerville, but the heyday was over. When the miners left, her business interests collapsed.

After 1875, Florence Wilson dropped out of sight, and little is known of her later years. Her legacy is one of a self-made woman who was warm, capable and energetic, and who broke the barriers of her class, the expectations of her forefathers and the wishes of those who wanted to place her in compliant domesticity as she stepped off the boat.

S. MARIA DUREN (CLARA MARIA DUREN)

There is an unsolved mystery surrounding the life of Maria Duren in British Columbia and it had everything to do with love.

Within days of his having jumped ship, Dr. John Chipp was hard at work; he had been the *Tynemouth*'s surgeon, a well-liked member of the ship's company. As a man of good conscience, Chipp's decision could not have been an easy one, *unless* there was something more — a now-or-never opportunity. It seems there was.

Almost nothing is known of Maria Duren — not her age, class or background — except that she was a passenger on the *Tynemouth*, and more than likely met Dr. Chipp while he was caring for Elizabeth Buchanan. A clandestine meeting between John and Maria would hardly have been possible on the vessel due to the chaperones. Did Elizabeth Buchanan's illness create a context where a new love might have blossomed?

John Chipp did very well in the Cariboo. He was considered by most a better surgeon than the other physician, Dr. Bell, and he soon found himself spearheading a committee to build Barkerville's first hospital.

It is known that during his early days in Barkerville, Dr. Chipp left on several occasions to visit Victoria. Was he wooing Maria Duren, who was toiling away in some upper-class household or teaching its children? It is known that Dr. Chipp brought his new wife, who was from Victoria, to Barkerville and that in the course of time, she bore him four healthy children.

In 1894, his beloved wife died in England. The formal announcement read simply:

> Clara Maria, wife of John Chipp, MD of Nicola, and mother of Mrs. W. Dewdney of Vernon, deeply mourned.[3]

Was Clara Maria the S. Maria Duren of the *Tynemouth*? Limited as the facts are, a *Tynemouth* genealogist was inclined to believe that "S. Maria Duren possibly married Dr. John Chipp(s)."[4]

Emma Lazenby

She was born in the small East Yorkshire parish of Bubwith in 1843. Growing up, she had seen the effects of England's Poor Laws, then witnessed the mass exodus of her kin and kind to the cotton mills of Lancashire, only to observe the destitution wrought by their closing years later. For Emma, Methodism offered a solution.

The Methodists had taken to forming temperance clubs after decades of government indifference had driven the poor and dispossessed of England's mid-northern counties to drink.

The Wesleyan Methodist missionaries were firmly rooted in Victoria when Emma arrived in January 1863. On Sunday, January 8, barely a week after arriving in the colony, Emma went to her first service in the Methodist Church on Pandora Street. She remained committed to its congregation and its ideals for the rest of her life.

Within a year Emma Lazenby was becoming something of an institution herself. Her first mission was among the children. The *Daily Colonist* noted, "She was one of the most able Sunday-School teachers in the life of Methodism in Victoria."[5] It was inevitable that through her work she would be drawn to someone who also had a strong sense of Wesleyan community activism.

David Spencer was a Welshman and a Methodist. In 1862, at 25, he had arrived in Victoria like so many of his mining brethren seeking gold and a new life. It took him less than a year to realize that the gold veins of the Fraser or the Cariboo were not for him. Somehow by Christmas he had scraped out of the earth enough money to return to Victoria, and within a month he had opened a modest bookshop and library on Government Street.

Angered by the numbers, the profits and the indifference of those who sold spirits, David Spencer joined a loose association of temperance organizers among the congregation of the Victoria Methodist Church, and it was there that he met Emma. They were married in the same church three years later on June 3, 1867. The marriage and the bookshop flourished, so much so that by 1873, David Spencer and an associate, William Denny, pooled their resources to open Victoria House, a dry-goods store. With men's flannel suits selling for three dollars, and tweed suits for four, the Spencers soon became very rich. With a final complement of 13 children of their own, they had to be.

In spite of the fine mansion near the residence of Sir James Douglas, which the Spencers built in 1885, they never forgot their commitment to temperance and the social gospel.

Emma Spencer was eventually designated "Superintendent of Social Purity."[6] She was in charge of establishing a refuge, a halfway house, in Victoria "to reclaim the fallen and shelter the friendless of our own sex."[7] In 1889 she was elected president of the Victoria Women's Christian Temperance Union. Under her tutelage, the refuge home gained a maternity ward, and many of its residents were found work in the community. A campaign was begun to create a women's wing at the Royal Jubilee Hospital. During her tenure, Emma Spencer prudently steered the WCTU away from growing public criticism. Though David Spencer was soon to become head of a large retail empire, Spencer's Limited, Emma remained close to her refuge home project right up to the end of the First World War.

In 1918, Dominion Prohibition became law, and Emma Spencer was elected honorary president of the Victoria Woman's Christian Temperance Union. Fate had saved her from the alleyways of Manchester that consumed so many of her kind, and she had spent her life trying to protect those she found abandoned in Victoria from a similar end. Marrying well, she might just as easily not have bothered, but she did, and it made a difference. Emma Spencer died at 91 in 1934.

LOUISA TOWNSEND AND CHARLOTTE TOWNSEND

The story of the Townsend sisters stands in contrast to the deprivation suffered by most of the other young women who undertook the voyage on the *Tynemouth*. Although they denied being members of the "sixty marriageable lassies"[8] sponsored by the Columbia Mission Society, the work they did and the liaisons they made in Victoria mark them both as quintessential, conservative English gentlewomen of the period. Their lives were as far from the raucous saloons of Barkerville or the salvation halls of temperance in Victoria as they could possibly get.

From the beginning, the Townsend sisters were bred into a life of privilege. Born into an upper-class English family of ten children, their childhood had all the advantages of their class.

> We had a lovely home and kind parents. We were taught what all properly brought up girls were supposed to know which included music and French. We never had to do any domestic work.[9]

Both expected Victoria to be much like England, and as Louisa noted, "We thought we should find most of the comforts of home."[10]

Genteel to the core, the Townsend sisters thought the girls destined for the colonial and matrimonial market-place an "odd assortment"[11] and frowned upon those who chose to wash themselves and their linen in front of the gawking hordes as soon as HMS *Forward* had landed them in James Bay. "My sister and I," said Louisa, "were in no such extremity. We had worn our old clothes on shipboard. In fact, we had given nightdresses and other things to some of the passengers, and before we landed we simply thrust our old clothes through the porthole. When we arrived, we had quite new garments, and our trunks were full of lovely things."[12]

Old family friends, the Pringles, met the Townsend sisters in Victoria and almost immediately took them to their home in a settlement "somewhere beyond New Westminster."[13] The house was drafty and cold, and Louisa slept in a garret that leaked. Though virile young settlers and sappers often paraded in front of the Pringles' house in the hope of a glimpse of the two sisters, Louisa reported crying herself to sleep many nights out of sheer loneliness. The adventure of travelling up the Fraser River, as Florence Wilson might have done, to see first-hand the men, the diggings and the shantytowns was an option or opportunity they simply did not entertain.

Louisa and Charlotte stayed with the Pringle family for three months before returning to Victoria. There they were overwhelmed by winter rains and mud. Sunday service in Christ Church Cathedral demanded they both carry short planks to be "put down in front of us to step on or we should have gone in over our boots."[14]

Daunted at first by the strange, rough life on a harsh and frightening frontier, the Townsend sisters adapted with an enduring grace and a natural kindness.

> One day I remember, when I was out walking, I met a girl who was soon to be married. I had on a lovely dress, very fashionable, and a pretty hat, and lace mitts. I did not know this girl very well, but she stopped me.
>
> "You've got a nice dress there," she said, "much nicer than anything I have in my trousseau. I wish you would be a bridesmaid at my wedding." I was astonished and amused, but I agreed."[15]

In time, Louisa's and Charlotte's circle gradually widened. Louisa went to the Pidwells of Humboldt Street and Charlotte found a position teaching music. J. T. Pidwell was a staunch Methodist; his daughters were spoiled and did not wish to learn from an Anglican. Louisa did not stay long, and her decision to move to "Maplehurst," the Rhodes estate, changed her life completely.

Rhodes and Janion were well-known auctioneers and merchants in Victoria in the 1860s. Henry Rhodes built his famous estate on land near the intersection of Blanshard and Princess streets. Maplehurst became the social centre of the Victoria elite when George Walkem, friend of Amor De Cosmos, married Sophie, daughter of Henry Rhodes, in 1871.

Louisa was at Maplehurst when unofficial government garden parties and military balls were putting the place high on the social agenda of the "ruling" class, and it was through her association with the noted household that she met the man who was destined to become her husband.

Edward Mallandaine's father was the Governor of Singapore. A true child of the Raj, Edward was born in India of English parents, and educated in Paris. He had arrived in Victoria just at the start of the Fraser River Gold Rush when the place was little more than a city of tents; he was a widower when he asked Louisa to her first real ball at Government House. Fussy and excited about what to wear she noted, "I bought a whole bolt of tarleton and made it [the dress] myself."[16] She and Edward danced the night away in drawing rooms so large, she might well have been in a Wiltshire country estate. They were married in 1873.

Months later, Charlotte Townsend married Alfred Allatt Townsend (same family name, but not related) whom she met at St. John's Church. Charlotte asked Charles Redfern, by then a very successful city jeweller, to be Alfred Townsend's best man. The sisters lived within blocks of each other as part of the Victoria establishment for the next 60 years. Several of their children remained prominent in Victoria until the 1950s.

The sisters broke no social barriers, and adhered strongly to the rigid social code that made Victoria more English than the English. Both were lucky, and were gracious enough to know it.

JANE ANNE SAUNDERS

Jane Saunders went into domestic service almost as soon as she arrived on the *Tynemouth*. Mrs. Chambers, her first employer, was lucky in that at 20, Jane was the quintessence of working-class resolve. Soon trusted, Jane noted with discretion the comings and goings in the Chambers household, but it didn't take long for her to notice the confident, bushy-whiskered Irishman who came round regularly to the back kitchen door.

Samuel Nesbitt had given up on the goldfields. He realized early that the road to the good life was not necessarily achieved through back-breaking labour at the sluice-boxes, but might be found in providing nourishment for those who did. By the time the *Tynemouth* arrived in 1862, he had taken what little gold his poke contained and was in Victoria up to his arms in more wholesome dough. He opened a bakery.

Sam was good at the baking business; the customers in his shop, at the corner of Yates and Broad streets, liked his pilot bread and his broad Irish humour. An early specialty, his hard-tack biscuits sold readily to the navy in Esquimalt.

Shrewdly, Sam advertised himself as baker to "Her Majesty's Navy" and thereby gained the notice and the business of the matrons of the elegant homes in the city. Jane Saunders met him as he made his daily rounds to the service entrance of the family home she served, with his arms full of bread and a voice full of charm. Jane was immediately smitten.

In April 1863, barely seven months after Jane Saunders stepped off the *Tynemouth*, the *British Colonist* published this announcement:

On the 16th Instant at Woodvine Cottage, the residence of W. P. Sayward, by the Rev. E. Cridge, Mr. Samuel Nesbitt of

Victoria to Miss Jane Anne Saunders, late of Highbury, London, England.[17]

Jane and Samuel worked well together and their business prospered, so they were able to build "Holly Lodge," the Nesbitt home on Cormorant Street. Holly trees imported from England made the grounds feel a little like the old country. After 11 years, the Nesbitts moved to ten acres of land on Cadboro Bay Road. On a hill overlooking the sea they built "Erin Hall" in the style of an Irish country manor. When Samuel died at 42 in 1881, Jane took over the business. The bakery flourished.

Some of their descendants became notable citizens in Victoria. Grandson James Knight Nesbitt was a well-known columnist for the Victoria *British Colonist* and his popular articles on the old families of the city remain as a fitting homage to the lives of his pioneering kin.

Martha Clay

Martha Clay arrived on the *Robert Lowe* and the man she married, Joseph Akerman, so one story goes, arrived on the *Tynemouth*. Joseph Akerman was born in the rolling hills of Wiltshire, where his family had been tenant farmers for generations. At 17 in 1862, he saw an opportunity to do better than simply becoming one more yeoman tiller of another man's soil. After a short stint as a longshoreman in New Westminster, Joseph opened a market garden near the site of the Legislative Buildings in Victoria. On a hunting venture to Salt Spring Island, Joseph found the land of his dreams.

The Clay sisters, Martha, Emma and Fannie, had come out together. Unemployed mill-workers from the midlands, they had convinced Maria Rye that their close relationship would be an asset in British Columbia. They had survived Cape Horn together;

now Martha faced another whirlwind all her own. The determined young market gardener with land-holding dreams needed a wife, and suddenly there she was.

On May 14, 1863, just four months after the *Robert Lowe* let go its anchor in Esquimalt Harbour, Martha Clay and Joseph Akerman were married. They honeymooned in their valley on Salt Spring Island, and became the first white family to settle permanently on the island. By 1895, the Akermans had three sons and five daughters, a 300-tree orchard and a thriving cattle and sheep farm of some 355 acres.

As of 1998, Joseph and Martha's descendants numbered well over 125. A yeoman farmer and a Manchester mill-worker did well by the bride-ships.

MARY MACDONALD

Mary Macdonald married up. She was a domestic, and Peter Leech was probably the most significant scientist/surveyor to settle in British Columbia. He joined the Ordinance Survey of the Royal Engineers in England in 1855 and came out to New Westminster in 1859 as part of Colonel Moody's corps. The Hudson's Bay Company brought him to Victoria where he met Mary Macdonald in 1868.

Not much is known of Mary, who had spent ten years in Victoria before she met Peter. Peter rose through the ranks of the Hudson's Bay Company and in 1872 became head of the company's post in Esquimalt. It was during this time that he built a large house for his wife and daughter overlooking Beacon Hill.

Mary died in 1892. Peter Leech quit the company and returned to private practice. He simplifed astronomical tables, and surveyed townsites such as Bella Coola. When his daughter died suddenly in 1899, Leech was devastated, and died later the same year.

EMMA TAMMADGE

If Emma Tammadge's voyage out to British Columbia on the *Tynemouth* was a trip to remember, then her husband's trek to Victoria, overland from Upper Canada, was the very stuff of legend. Richard Henry survived the famous Overlanders journey though several of his friends drowned canoeing down the Fraser.

In Victoria, he met Emma Tammadge. He also met Jeremiah Griffiths, because he worked as a longshoreman on Griffiths's Hudson's Bay Company wharf. It is uncertain but likely that Griffiths helped him to obtain the post of clerk in a Wharf Street warehouse.

Richard took Emma to Burrard Inlet when he was offered the job of manager of the Hastings Mill store. As Vancouver grew up around him, he became a member of the Granville School Board and served as a Vancouver councillor in 1887-88. Emma was on the wharf in Burrard Inlet when Lord and Lady Dufferin paid a visit to Vancouver in September 1876, and noted Lady Dufferin's interest in native people. Emma bore Richard four daughters and as the sawmill prospered in the 1880s, the family began to acquire substantial land in the growing city. When Vancouver incorporated, Richard served as a justice of the peace and became president of the Board of Trade. Looking out to the North Shore wilderness from the family home above Hastings Mill, Emma must have pondered the distance she had come. From a bride-ships' emigrant domestic servant to one of Vancouver's first citizens, Emma Tammadge would never have believed her own story.

MINNIE GILLAN

Minnie Gillan is immortalized on a bronze plaque on the seawall overlooking the inner harbour in Victoria. Placed there in 1957, it reads:

The *Tynemouth*, 1862, with Minnie Gillan (Mrs. John Cox, 1869)
Presented by her descendants.

A London orphan, raised by the sisters of St. Margaret in Grinstead, Minnie Gillan was as devout as she was poor. After her initial visit to Christ Church Cathedral with the other *Tynemouth* girls, Minnie was drawn back largely by its friendly pastor. Reverend Cridge wasn't afraid to modify the service in order to reach his congregation and he was different from the dour, chiding moralists such as Reverend Scott and Bishop Hills. Minnie used to wander the grounds of Christ Church, with its wild flowers and quiet cemetery, and often lingered there after Sunday services, a brief respite from the long hours and hard labour of her life as a domestic servant.

John Cox was the cemetery keeper at Christ Church and Minnie used to see him, occasionally at first, tending the grounds, chatting with Reverend Cridge, and sitting, always in the same pew at the back, during Wednesday night evensong. Seven years after she arrived, Minnie Gillan married John Cox. When Reverend Cridge left the Anglican Church, John and Minnie and most of the rest of his congregation at Christ Church went with him. John and Minnie Cox served Reverend Cridge and the episcopal movement for the rest of their lives.

Minnie eventually bore John nine children — five daughters and four sons. She predeceased her beloved husband by 15 years, and was buried in Ross Bay Cemetery on December 2, 1911.

MARY HODGES
Perhaps one of the more notable women of the bride-ships enterprise to have graced Victoria with her presence was Mary Hodges. Not only did she *not* fit the stereotype of respectability

and deference that the Columbia Emigration Society organizers had envisaged, she held the whole ideological movement up to public contempt. Mary Hodges used the scheme as no other sponsored woman and was neither shamed nor transformed by her actions. She was one of those women on the *Tynemouth* whom Frederick Whymper referred to as having "been there before."[18] More indignantly, Commander Verney thought that she was "*thoroughly bad* and must have been so before leaving England."[19] No doubt she was, for everything about Mary Hodges was a lie, including her name.

Mary Hodges was never placed into domestic service when she arrived in Victoria. Instead, she fell in with Dora and Lizzie Freidman, the two dubious daughters of a Johnson Street boot and shoe dealer. With them, she frequented various dance halls in the city, and was known to have sexual relations with at least one miner from the Cariboo. Suddenly, in March 1864, she married. It was a troubled relationship right from the start.

On May 13, 1864, Mary was invited to Herman Schultz's house where both he and another shopkeeper, Jasper Trickey plied her with liquor, and then assaulted her. She charged them both with rape.

In court, Mary stated, "I came out from England in the steamer *Tynemouth* under the name of my stepfather Hodges; I was married here under my proper name Hurst." She went on, "My sister wrote me my name, she said I was not a christian, and I changed the name of Mary Hodges to Esther Hurst."[20] But that, too, was a lie; Mary Hodges was not only Esther Hurst, she was Esther Meiss. Mary Hodges was Jewish.

Mary denied that she had a key to Schultz's house and had been there numerous times before, and disputed that she was seen at Trickey's cottage before and after the alleged rape. She admitted, however, to being intimate with a Mr. Jacob, stealing from her husband, and not telling him of the alleged assault until two weeks after it happened. The jury acquitted Schultz and Trickey, who left the court immediately, while Esther (Mary) Meiss indulged in "un-lady-like epithets while expressing her indignation against all concerned."[21]

In her associations with Jacob, Schultz, Morris, the Freidman sisters and many others of Victoria's Jewish community, Esther Meiss was obviously aware of her own origins. She had changed her name to give herself an advantage in an essentially English-only colony that felt itself threatened by outsiders. The mandarins of the bride-ships enterprise wanted only pure, white women for their venture, so a pure, white woman Mary Hodges would become. What became of her after the trial is unknown.

MARGARET FAUSSETT

Margaret Faussett came out on the *Tynemouth* as a governess, became a teacher, married a teacher and influenced the man who shaped early public education in British Columbia more than any other. John Jessop arrived in Victoria in no less a heroic fashion than Margaret Faussett. He walked to Victoria from Fort Garry in 1859 and he soon opened a private, non-sectarian school in Victoria's old Assembly Hall on View Street. When the Vancouver Island colony's public-school system was inaugurated in 1862, Jessop's venture in private education was doomed.

John Jessop was lucky; by the time British Columbia entered Confederation in 1871, he had met and married Margaret Faussett, who had become a teacher in Jessop's school as soon as the opportunity presented itself.

The Jessops felt strongly about the efficacy of a public education system that would be free from ecclesiastical underpinnings and together they presented to the province's provincial secretary the plan for British Columbia's first Public School Act. Appointed

Superintendent of Education for British Columbia for his efforts, Jessop then outlined the principles for free, non-sectarian schools in the province. Together, the Jessops worked to enshrine those principles of freedom denied to whole classes of citizens in the country they had gladly left behind.

AUGUSTA JANE MORRIS AND EMILY ANN MORRIS

Augusta Jane and Emily Ann were landed in New Westminster on Saturday, September 20. They didn't have time to even think about life up-country for they were courted and married almost where they stood, and the Lower Mainland became their home for life.

William Bentley was a young English soldier who had survived the Crimean War. Not wishing to go through another Balaclava, he joined the Royal Engineers and, along with 150 others, arrived in New Westminster in 1859. Augusta liked the rugged good looks of the worldly young man in uniform she danced with at the Engineers' Christmas Ball and William was taken with Augusta. They married, pre-empted land offered to the Royal Engineers who remained in the mainland colony after the company disbanded in 1863 and farmed together in the Fraser Valley for the rest of their lives.

Through her sister's husband, Emily Ann met Joseph Farr, a young blacksmith in New Westminster. They married, moved to Chilliwack and opened a livery stable. For 30 years, Emily Ann raised a family, while Joseph's business prospered. When Joseph died in 1901, Emily Ann decided to remain. In her 50s she met and married D. C. McGillivray and stayed in Chilliwack.

FRANCIS CURTIS AND ISABEL CURTIS

Mother and daughter, the Curtises came out together on the *Tynemouth*. Widowed at 30 in London, Mrs. Curtis was still fit and good-looking and convinced the Columbia Emigration Society that she was young enough to start again. Her plan was to send for her two sons, whom she had left with a relative in London, as soon as she was settled and had saved the fare; at 13, little Isabel was fast becoming a beauty, so Francis thought she had better bring her blossoming daughter with her and satisfied the committee that the two of them would be an asset to the familial goals of the bride-ships venture.

Sisters were common among the *Tynemouth* women, but mothers with children were not; they had to prove their suitability. The two who did so swore upon their lives that age and experience would give them an edge. Eliza Reynolds pleaded with the committee to allow her to bring her infant son; she argued that left alone in a London orphanage, he would surely die for want of proper care. Francis asserted to the committee that Isabel could easily be preyed upon by men, or worse, become a wanton woman, without careful parental supervision. The committee had mercy on the two mothers, recognizing the dangers of the forced abandonment of their children; they also hoped that their possible marriages would create two instant families, a goal of the Columbia Mission.

Isabel was one of the youngest passengers on the *Tynemouth*, but she was almost a woman and by far the most beautiful person on board. With long, golden tresses and a pale English complexion, she turned the heads of the officers and crew alike. She was so striking that when she stepped off the longboat of HMS *Forward* in James Bay she had already been "advised to wear a veil when walking the streets of the rowdy, gold-mad town."[22]

In four years Isabel matured into one of the most attractive young women in the colony. She had fallen in love with a handsome young Royal Navy officer on station in Esquimalt, but Francis thought her daughter could do far better than marry a lowly naval man who was likely to be posted all over the empire. Dutifully, Isabel gave up her uniformed young man and married Thomas George Askew, a wealthy sawmill operator in Chemainus, a man of whom mother approved.

Widowed in 1880, Isabel was left deeply in debt. Much to the chagrin of the major shareholders, who included her mother's husband, William Boucherat, she decided to run the mill herself. Facing continued hardship, she applied for a liquor licence to turn part of her Chemainus home into a pub, but was dissuaded by negative public opinion and opened a small store and post office instead. For five years Isabel and her eight children lived a hand-to-mouth existence.

By 1885, Isabel had saved enough to build a house in Victoria and moved there with the children. That same year, when business in his Chemainus operation took a nosedive, Boucherat decided to sell out. Francis was ill and she convinced Isabel that she and her stepfather should simply move into Isabel's new home, "The Junipers," on Pemberton Road and share expenses. As Francis's health failed, she became more and more hysterical. The horrific voyage out on the *Tynemouth* had so shaken her that she would not allow her two boys in England to make the ocean crossing to see her after an absence of almost 25 years. To risk the trip home herself was out of the question. Francis never did see her sons again and she died in Victoria in 1888.

At 33, Isabel was still a good-looking woman and her widowed stepfather leered and prowled about the house. Time and time again William asked Isabel to marry him, and when that failed, he turned to threats.

When William finally understood that he was not going to gain Isabel's heart, he turned his attentions to Julia, her eldest daughter. However, Julia detested his advances and William finally slunk away to California with another woman.

Isabel Curtis had learned life's lessons the hard way. Finally independent of those who would control her life, she remained in her home and raised her children alone, but it was not easy. Her youngest son, Walter, had become a paymaster for a lumber mill in the interior. While carrying a large sum of money to Seattle, he was attacked and killed by thugs, and tossed into Puget Sound. His body was never found. Isabel's youngest daughter, Edith Isabella, died in infancy. Courageous and beautiful to the end, Isabel died on October 12, 1905; she was only 56.

The women who came to British Columbia on the bride-ships gained lives of adventure and material wealth that they could not even have dreamed of in the grimy streets of Manchester, the crofters' huts of Yorkshire, the orphanages of East Grinstead or even the terraces of Highgate. Beyond that, their lives were personal expressions of a flexibility and freedom of choice that simply were not available to them in their unkind and confined homeland. Though the loftier aims of the bride-ships experiment were not achieved, the women themselves, no doubt, enjoyed richer lives.

Endnotes

Chapter One: Liberalism and Squalor

1 Alfred Lord Tennyson. "In Memoriam." In T. Herbert Warren. *Poems of Tennyson, 1830-1870.* (Oxford: Oxford University Press, 1936) p. 392.

2 Minutes of "The City Meeting." In *The Third Report of the Columbia Mission.* 1862. p. 37.

3 *Ibid.*, p. 38.

4 *Ibid.*, p. 40. The clergyman's name was the Reverend Alexander Charles Garrett, and he became Principal of the Indian Mission in Victoria.

5 *Ibid.*, p. 41.

6 *Ibid.*, p. 42.

7 *Ibid.*, p. 43.

8 *Ibid.*

9 *Ibid.*, p. 52

10 *Ibid.*, p. 53.

11 The phrase is from "Jerusalem," the quintessential Victorian hymn. The sentence is a paraphrase of J. B. Priestly's famous denunciation of the 19th century. The actual phrase reads, "It had found a green and pleasant land and left a wilderness of dirty bricks." In Martin Weiner. *English Culture and the Decline of the Industrial Spirit, 1850-1980.* p. 124.

12 *Ibid.*, p. 24. The quotation is from Charles Dickens's *Our Mutual Friend.*

13 *Ibid.*, p. 78.

14 *Annual Report of the Columbia Mission.* 1861. p. 45.

15 James Hammerton. *Emigrant Gentlewomen.* p. 127.

16 Maria S. Rye. "The Colonies and their Requirements." In *The English Women's Review.* Vol. 8, No. 4, November, 1861, p. 165-171.

17 *Ibid.*, p. 171.

18 *The Times* of London. April 2, 1862.

19 *Ibid.,* April 11, 1862.

20 *Ibid.* The debate is especially well covered in Hammerton's *Emigrant Gentlewomen,* p. 128-129, but the critical letters to *The Times* of London include: April 2, 3, 11, 23, 24, 26, 28, 29, 1862.

21 *The Times* of London. April 7, 1862.

22 *Ibid.*

23 Sarah Crease. "Stray Letters on the Emigration Question." In *The English*

Woman's Journal. Vol. 8, No. 45, January 11, 1861, p. 241.
24 *Ibid.*

Chapter Two: Violence in the Black Canyons
1 Robert Service. *Collected Poems of Robert Service.* (New York: Dodd, Mead
   & Co., 1866), p. 48.
2 "Mapping the Frontier: Charles Wilson's Diary of the Survey of the 49th
   Parallel, While Secretary of the British Boundary Commission." In G.P.V.
   Akrigg and Helen Akrigg. *British Columbia Chronicle, 1847-1871.* p. 113.
3 John Keast Lord. "The Naturalist in Vancouver Island and British
   Columbia." In G.P.V. Akrigg and Helen Akrigg. *British Columbia
   Chronicle, 1847-1871.* p. 114.
4 Lundin Brown. "Lillooet Mission." In *Mission Life.* p. 561, 562.
5 Bruce Hutchison. *The Fraser.* (Toronto: Clarke, Irwin & Co., 1982), p. 7.
6 *British Colonist.* November 28, 1862.
7 *The British Columbian.* June 1, 1869. In Robin Fisher. *Contact and
   Conflict.* p. 104.
8 *Victoria Gazette.* August 20, 1858, p. 3. In today's currency, these amounts
   are multiplied by 15.
9 *Ibid.,* August 24, 1858, p. 3.
10 D. W. Higgins. *The Mystic Spring.* p. 48.
11 Charles Major. Letter home, September 20, 1859. In Robin Reid, ed.
   "Gold Rush Narratives." In *British Columbia Historical Quarterly.* Vol. 5,
   No. 3. July 1941. p. 230.
12 "Journal of Service of Lieutenant Charles William Wilson, R. E., with
   The Boundary Commisssion." Entry for August 2, 1858. British Columbia
   Archives.
13 Robin Reid, ed. "Gold Rush Narratives." In *British Columbia
   Historical Quarterly.* Vol. 5, No. 3. July 1941, p. 227. D.W. Higgins
   believed the population to be between 5,000 and 6,000. *The Mystic
   Spring.* p. 49.
14 D.W. Higgins. *The Mystic Spring.* p. 56.
15 W.B. Cheadle and C. W. Wentworth Fitzwilliam. In Branwen Patenaude.
   Trails to Gold. (Victoria: Horsdal & Schubart, 1995), p. 17.
16 Branwen Patenaude. *Trails to Gold.* p. 29.
17 *British Colonist.* December 20, 1859. p. 3.
18 *Ibid.*

Chapter Three: Prophets and Pilgrims

1 John Bunyan. "To Be a Pilgrim." From *Hymns Ancient & Modern Revised*. (London: William Clowes and Sons Ltd., 1950). No. 293.

2 John Sheepshanks made this comment about Hills in his diary. In Frank Peake. *The Anglican Church in British Columbia*. p. 42.

3 Joan Weir. *Catalysts and Watchdogs:* ... p. 19.

4 *Ibid.*, p. 148.

5 *Ibid.*, p. 147.

6 D. Wallace Duthie, ed. "A Bishop in the Rough, the Diaries of John Sheepshanks." In Lyndon Grove. *Pacific Pilgrims*. p. 21.

7 *Ibid.*, p. 21.

8 *Ibid.*, p. 22.

9 George Hills. "A Sermon ..." In Robin Fisher. *Contact and Conflict*. p. 124.

10 *Ibid.*, p. 563.

11 Lundin Brown. "Lillooet Mission." In *Mission Life*. p. 563.

12 D. Wallace Duthie, ed. "A Bishop in the Rough." p. 63.

13 *Ibid.*

14 *Ibid.*, p. 67.

15 *Ibid.*, p. 68-69.

16 *Ibid.*, p. 89.

17 *Ibid.*, p. 93.

18 *Ibid.*

19 Lundin Brown. *British Columbia, An Essay*. (New Westminster: Royal Engineers Press, 1863), p. 53.

20 Lundin Brown. "Lillooet Mission." In *Mission Life*. p. 564.

21 *Ibid.*, p. 565.

22 *Ibid.*, p. 564.

23 *Ibid.*

24 *Ibid.*

25 *Ibid.*

26 *Ibid.*, p. 566.

27 *The British Columbian*. September 12, 1863.

28 *Ibid.*

29 Lundin Brown. *British Columbia, An Essay*. p. 53.

30 Brett Christophers. *Positioning the Missionary*. p. 61.

31 *British Colonist*. December 20, 1861, p. 3.

32 Lundin Brown. "Lillooet Mission." In *Mission Life*. p. 566.

Chapter Four: False Starts and Faint Hope

1 Allan Pritchard, ed. *The Vancouver Island Letters* ... p. 75.

2 *Ibid.*, p. 74.

3 *Ibid.*, p. 9.

4 *Ibid.*, p. 34.

5 *Ibid.*, p. 35.

6 *Ibid.*

7 *Ibid.*, p. 33.

8 *Ibid.*, p. 10.

9 Jean Usher. *William Duncan of Metlakatla.* p. 27.

10 Richard Charles Mayne. *Four Years in British Columbia and Vancouver Island.* (London: John Murray, 1862; reprint, Toronto: S. R. publishers, 1969), p. 76.

11 *British Colonist.* November 30, 1861. p. 3.

12 *Ibid.*

13 *Ibid.*

14 Jane Rendell. "Friendship and Politics: ..." In Susan Mendies, ed. *Sexuality and Subjugation.* p. 160

15 *Ibid.*, p. 161.

16 *Ibid.*, p. 162.

17 *British Colonist.* May 23, 1861. p. 3.

18 *Ibid.*

19 *Ibid.*, May 21, 1861, p. 3.

20 *Ibid.*, May 31, 1861. p. 3.

21 *Ibid.*

22 Adele Perry. *On the Edge of Empire.* p. 148.

23 *British Colonist.* May 31, 1861, p. 3.

24 Allan Pritchard, ed. *The Vancouver Island Letters* ... p. 79.

25 *Ibid.*, p. 80

26 *Ibid.*

27 *Ibid.*

28 *Ibid.*

29 *Ibid.*

30 *British Colonist.* September 11, 1862. p, 3.

31 *Ibid.*

32 William Silvester. "Victoria's Brideships." In *True West*, November 1985. p. 42.

33 *British Colonist*. September 12, 1862. p. 3.

34 *Ibid.,* September 15, 1862. p. 3.

35 John Malcolm Brinnin. *The Sway of the Grand Salon*. p. 8.

36 Andrew Hassam. *No Privacy for Writing*. p. xxii.

37 *British Colonist*. September 19, 1862. p. 3.

38 *Ibid.*

39 *Ibid.,* September 22, 1862. p. 3.

40 Allan Pritchard, ed. *The Vancouver Island Letters* ... p. 91.

Chapter Five: The Voyage from Hell

 1 Andrew Hassam. *No Privacy for Writing*. p.xxv.

 2 *The Times* of London. May 9, 1862. p. 2.

 3 Charles Redfern. "Reminiscences of Long Sea Voyage Sixty Years Ago."

 4 *Ibid.,* p. 20.

 5 Frederick Whymper. *Travel and Adventure* ... p. 22.

 6 *Tynemouth* Passenger Contract Ticket No. 13. Issued to Charles and
   Robert Green. May 5, 1862. BC Archives, File No. J G T97.

 7 Charles Redfern. "Reminiscences."

 8 *Ibid.*

 9 Frederick Whymper. *Travel and Adventure* ... p. 22.

10 Lady Jane Franklin, widow of Arctic explorer Sir John Franklin, was in
   Victoria in 1861. She and the Rev. Scott never actually met, but she did
   write of him in her diary. See Andrew Forest Muir. "William Richard Scott."
   In *British Columbia Historical Quarterly*. July-October 1956. p. 167-168.

11 Frederick Whymper. *Travel and Adventure* ... p. 23.

12 *Ibid.*

13 *Ibid.,* p. 24.

14 There are two eyewitness versions of the mutiny aboard the *Tynemouth,* by
   Charles Redfern and Frederick Whymper. Redfern's account was written
   some 60 years later as a reminiscence, and Whymper's was published nine
   years after the voyage. Redfern claims there were two insurrections, the
   latter violent one being due to crew still angry over the previous
   confinement of some their mates. Whymper, however, mentions only one
   insurrection, the violent one. I have chosen to accept Redfern's more
   distant account of two outbursts, because it describes the rebellion in
   greater chronological detail. As well, Whymper is careful of what he says
   against the powers that be.

15 Frederick Whymper. *Travel and Adventure* ... p. 24.

16 *Ibid.*, p. 25.

17 *Ibid.*

18 Charles Redfern. "Reminiscences."

19 Frederick Whymper. *Travel and Adventure* ... p. 26.

20 Charles Redfern. "Reminiscences."

21 Frederick Whymper. *Travel and Adventure* ... p. 26

22 *Ibid.*

23 *Ibid.*, p. 27

24 *Ibid.*

25 *Ibid.*

26 *British Colonist.* September 17, 1862. p. 3.

27 *Ibid.*

Chapter Six: The Arrival of the *Tynemouth*

1 *The Daily Press.* September 18, 1862. p. 3. The *British Colonist* ran the same ad September 20, 1862.

2 *British Colonist.* September 11, 1862. p. 3.

3 *Ibid.*, September 6, 1862. p. 3.

4 *Ibid.*, September 22, 1862. p. 3.

5 *Ibid.*, September 15, 1862. p. 3.

6 *Ibid.*, September 19, 1862. p. 3.

7 *Ibid.*

8 *Ibid.*

9 *Ibid.*

10 *Ibid.*

11 *Ibid.*

12 *Ibid.*

13 *Ibid.*

14 Allan Pritchard, ed. *The Vancouver Island Letters* ... p. 89.

15 *Ibid.*

16 *The Daily Press.* September 24, 1862. p. 3.

17 *Ibid.*

18 *Ibid.*, September 19, 1862. p. 3.

19 Charles Hayward. Unpublished Diary. September 19, 1862.

20 *Ibid.* Hayward noted the number of ladies from the *Tynemouth* as 61.

21 *Ibid.*

22 *British Colonist*. January 25, 1976. p. 10.

23 *Ibid.*

24 Allan Pritchard, ed. *The Vancouver Island Letters* ... p. 90.

25 *Ibid.*, p. 115.

26 *Ibid.*

27 *Ibid.*

28 *The Daily Press*. September 21, 1862. p. 3.

29 John Hosie, ed. *Pioneer Women of Vancouver Island*. p. 150.

30 Allan Pritchard, ed. *The Vancouver Island Letters* ... p. 88.

31 *The British Columbian*. September 24, 1862. p. 3.

32 Allan Pritchard, ed. *The Vancouver Island Letters* ... p. 91.

33 *Ibid.*

34 *The Daily Press*. September 18, 1862. p. 3.

35 *Ibid.*

36 *Ibid.*, September 22, 1862. p. 3.

37 *Ibid.*

38 Allan Pritchard, ed. *The Vancouver Island Letters* ... p. 88.

39 *Ibid.*, p. 90.

40 *Ibid.*

41 *Ibid.*

42 George Hills, Journal. January 1- June 10, 1863. (Transcript) Anglican Diocese of New Westminster. p. 30.

43 *British Colonist*. September 19, and 20, 1862; *The Daily Press*. September 21, 1862.

44 *British Colonist*. September 22, 1862.

45 Charles Hayward. Unpublished Diary. September 21, 1862.

46 *British Colonist*. March 14, 1861. p. 3.

47 Andrew Forest Muir. "William Richard Scott." In *British Columbia Historical Quarterly*. July-October, 1956. p. 167-168.

48 *Ibid.*, p. 183. The charges were laid by an American Congregational missionary, Luther Halsey Gulick.

49 *The Daily Press*. September 22, 1862. p. 3.

50 *British Colonist*. September 22, 1862. p.3.

51 *Ibid.*, September 25, 1862. p. 3.

52 *The Daily Press*. September 24, 1862. p. 3.

53 *Ibid.* The usual contract for a merchant seaman was for three years with a commercial vessel such as the *Tynemouth*.

54 *Ibid.*
55 *British Colonist.* September 27, 1862. p. 3.
56 Frederick Whymper. *Travel and Adventure.* p. 30.
57 *The Daily Press.* October 15, 1862. p. 3.

Chapter Seven: The *Robert Lowe*
1 *British Colonist.* January 12, 1863. p. 2.
2 *Ibid.*
3 *Ibid.*, p. 3.
4 *Ibid.*
5 *Ibid.*
6 *Ibid.*
7 *Ibid.*
8 *Ibid.*
9 *Ibid.*
10 *Ibid.*
11 *Ibid.*
12 *Ibid.*
13 *Ibid.*
14 *Ibid.*
15 *Ibid.*, January 17, 1863. p. 3.
16 *Ibid.*
17 *Ibid.*
18 *Ibid.*
19 J.S. Reader. *Life in Victorian England.* p. 121.
20 *British Colonist.* January 13, 1862. p. 3.
21 *Ibid.*
22 Allan Pritchard, ed. *The Vancouver Island Letters ...* p. 114.
23 *British Colonist.* January 13, 1862. p. 3.
24 *Ibid.*
25 *Ibid.*
26 George Hills, Journal. January 1-June 10, 1863. (Transcript) Anglican Diocese of New Westminster. p. 5.
27 *The Victoria Daily Chronicle.* June 28, 1864.

Chapter Eight: The Wife Experiment Reconsidered
1 "M." Anonymous doggerel noted by J.T. Jones. "Cleanly, Well Built,

Pretty Young Things." In *British Colonist*. May 24, 1962. p. 28.

2 Letter from the Rev. Cridge to Gov. James Douglas, July 14, 1863. BC Archives. Douglas Correspondence (incoming).

3 *British Colonist*. January 25, 1869. p. 3.

4 *Ibid*.

5 Bishop Hills. In *The Sixth Report of the Columbia Mission*. p. 19.

6 *The British Columbian*. June 20, 1868. p. 3.

7 *British Colonist*. March 13, 1869. p. 3.

8 *Ibid.*, April 14, 1869. p. 3.

9 *Ibid.*, April 29, 1869. p. 3.

10 *Ibid.*, February 4, 1869. p. 3.

11 *Ibid.*, August 17, 1869. p. 3.

12 *Ibid.*, August 21, 1869. p. 3.

13 *Ibid.*, June 15, 1870. p. 3.

14 *Ibid*.

15 *Ibid.*, April 26, 1869. p. 3.

16 M. Jeanne Peterson. "The Victorian Governess: Status and Incongruence in Family and Society." In *Victorian Studies*, Vol. 14, No. 1, September 1970. p. 8.

17 Maria Rye. "Emigration of Educated Women." In James Hammerton. *Emigrant Gentlewomen*. p. 52.

18 *The Times* of London. July 28, 1862.

19 Brett Christophers. *Positioning the Missionary*. p. 56-57.

20 James Hammerton. *Emigrant Gentlewomen*. p. 139.

Chapter Nine: Diffusion

1 A.H. Clough. "Say Not the Struggle Naught Availeth." In *The Oxford Book of English Verse*. #741.

2 Florence Wilson file. BC Archives.

3 James Nesbitt. "Dr. Chipp Came On Brideship." In *The Daily Colonist*. July 16, 1967. p. 4.

4 Jo Dunaway. "The Search for the Tynemouth Women." In *The British Columbia Genealogist*. Vol. 16, No. 4, December 1988.

5 *The Daily Colonist*. May 10, 1924.

6 Lyn Gough. *As Wise As Serpents*. p. 22.

7 *Ibid.*, p. 22.

8 Nancy De Bertrand Lugrin. "The Brideships." In John Hosie, ed. *The*

Pioneer Women of Vancouver Island. p. 146.

9 *The Daily Colonist.* March 23, 1924. p. 27.

10 *Ibid.*

11 *Ibid.*

12 *Ibid.*

13 *Ibid.*

14 *Ibid.*

15 Nancy De Bertrand Lugrin. "The Brideships." p. 151.

16 *Ibid.,* p. 159.

17 *British Colonist.* April 17, 1863.

18 Frederick Whymper. *Travel and Adventure* ... p. 23.

19 Allan Pritchard, ed. *The Vancouver Island Letters* ... p. 90.

20 Police Court Testimony. In Adele Perry. *On the Edge of Empire.* p. 179.

21 *British Colonist.* August 2, 1864. p. 3.

22 Elizabeth Forbes. *Wild Roses At Their Feet.* p. 111.

Bibliography

PUBLISHED SOURCES

Akrigg, G.P.V., Akrigg, Helen. *British Columbia Chronicle 1847-1871.* Vancouver: Discovery Press, 1977.

Allen, Harold. *Forty Years Journey: The Temperance Movement in British Columbia to 1900.* Victoria: Women's Temperance Committee, 1981.

Annual Report of the Columbia Mission. London: Rivingtons, 1860 on.

Bagshaw, Roberta, ed. *No Better Land, The 1860 Diaries of the Anglican Colonial Bishop George Hills.* Victoria: Sono Nis Press, 1996.

Brinnin, John Malcolm. *The Sway of the Grand Salon, A Social History of the North Atlantic.* New York: Delacorte Press, 1971.

Christophers, Brett. *Positioning the Missionary.* Vancouver: University of British Columbia Press, 1998.

Cobden-Unwin, L. *The Hungry Forties, Life under the Bread Tax.* London: T. Fisher Unwin, 1904.

Dietz, Frederick. *Political and Social History of England.* New York: Macmillan Co., 1945.

Forbes, Elizabeth. *Wild Roses at Their Feet.* Vancouver: British Columbia Centennial Committee, 1971.

Fisher, Robin. *Contact and Conflict: Indian-European Relations in British Columbia, 1774-1890.* Vancouver: University of British Columbia Press, 1977.

Gough, Lyn. *As Wise as Serpents.* Victoria: Swan Lake Publishing, 1988.

Gould, Jan. *Women of British Columbia.* Victoria: Hancock House, 1980.

Green, Valerie. *Above Stairs: Social Life in Upper-Class Victoria, 1843-1918.* Victoria: Sono Nis Press, 1995.

Grove, Lyndon. *Pacific Pilgrims.* Vancouver: Fforbez Publications, Committee of Anglican Diocese of New Westminster, 1966.

Hammerton, James. *Emigrant Gentlewomen.* London: Croon Helm Ltd., 1979.

Hassam, Andrew. *No Privacy for Writing. Shipboard Diaries, 1852-1879.* Melbourne: Melbourne University Press, 1995.

———. *Sailing to Australia.* Manchester: Manchester University Press, 1994.

Healey, Edna. *Lady Unknown, The Life of Angela Burdett Coutts.* London: Sidgwick and Jackson, 1978.

Higgins, D.W. *The Mystic Spring.* Toronto: William Briggs, 1904.

Horton, Diana. *Made of Gold, A Biography of Angela Burdett Coutts.* London: Hamish and Co.,1980.

Hosie, John, ed. *The Pioneer Women of Vancouver Island.* Victoria: Women's Canadian Club of Victoria, 1928.

Hutchison, Bruce. *The Fraser.* Toronto: Clarke, Irwin & Co., 1982.

Johnston, H.J.M. *British Emigration Policy 1815-1830.* Oxford: Clarendon Press, 1972.

Lay, Jackie. "To Columbia on the Tynemouth." In Latham, Barbara and Kess, Cathy, eds. *In Her Own Right: Selected Essays in Women's History in British Columbia.* Victoria: Camosun College, 1980.

Lundin Brown, Rev. R.C. "Lillooet Mission." In *Mission Life.* New York: Cassell, Petter and Galpin, 1870.

Mackie, Richard Somerset. *The Wilderness Profound, Victorian Life on the Gulf of Georgia.* Victoria: Sono Nis Press, 1995.

McNab, John. *They Went Forth.* Toronto: McClelland and Stewart, 1955.

Mendies, Susan, ed. *Sexuality and Subjugation.* London: Routledge and Co., 1989.

Peake, Frank. *The Anglican Church in British Columbia.* Vancouver: Mitchell Press, 1959.

Perry, Adele. *On the Edge of Empire; Gender, Race, and the Making of British Columbia, 1849-1871.* Toronto: University of Toronto Press, 2001.

Pethick, Derek. *Victoria, The Fort.* Vancouver: Mitchell Press, 1968.

_____. *Summer of Promise.* Victoria: Sono Nis Press, 1980.

Priestley, J.B. *Victoria's Heyday.* London: Heinemann and Co., 1972.

Pritchard, Allan, ed. *The Vancouver Island Letters of Edmund Hope Verney, 1862-1865.* Vancouver: University of British Columbia Press, 1996.

Reader, W.J. *Life in Victorian England.* London: B.T. Basford Ltd., 1967.

Redfern, Charles. "Reminiscences of Long Sea Voyage Sixty Years Ago." In *British Colonist.* September 17, 1922.

Shepperson, W. S. *British Emigration to North America. Projects and Opinions in the Early Victorian Period.* Oxford: Basil Blackwell, 1957.

Smart, William. *Economic Annals of the 19ᵗʰ Century. 1821-1830.* Vol. II. New York: Augustus Kelly, 1964.

Usher, Jean. *William Duncan of Metlakatla.* Ottawa: National Museum of Man, 1974.

Weiner, Martin. *English Culture and the Decline of the Industrial Spirit, 1850-1980.* Cambridge: Cambridge University Press, 1981.

Weir, Joan. *Catalysts and Watchdogs, B.C.'s Men of God 1836-1871.* Victoria: Sono Nis Press, 1995.

Whymper, Frederick. *Travel and Adventure in the Territory of Alaska.* New York: Harper & Brothers, 1871.

UNPUBLISHED SOURCES

Askew, Isabel. Letters. MS 2879, Box 6 File 10. British Columbia Archives.

Cridge, Edward. Letter to James Douglas. July 14, 1863. Douglas Correspondence (incoming) F306-3. British Columbia Archives.

Hayward, Charles. Diary. AD 741, Vol. 1, File 4. British Columbia Archives.

McCallum, Douglas. "Barkerville Theatre in Context." Unpublished MA thesis. University of British Columbia, 1981.

Tod, John. "History of New Caledonia and the Northwest Coast." Victoria: British

Columbia Archives, 1858.

Tynemouth File. J G T97 Contract Ticket issued to *Tynemouth* passengers Charles and Robert Green. British Columbia Archives.

Wilson, Florence. File. British Columbia Archives.

_____. File, R.I.C. Barkerville Historic Town Archives.

MAGAZINES

British Columbia Historical Quarterly
British Columbia Historical News
British Columbia Genealogist
The English Woman's Journal
The English Women's Review
Illustrated London News
Mission Life
Oregon Historical Quarterly
The Peoples Magazine
Times Colonist Islander
True West Magazine
Victorian Studies

NEWSPAPERS

The British Colonist
The British Columbian
The Cariboo Sentinel
The Daily Press
The Melbourne Argus
The New York Tribune
The Times, London
Victoria Daily Chronicle
Victoria Daily Colonist
The Victoria Gazette

Index

225